The Expert Authority Code:

How To Get Seen, Trusted and Paid For What You Already Know

Written by Christine Blosdale – The Expert Authority Coach®

DISCLAIMER

The information provided in this book is for educational and informational purposes only. While every effort has been made to ensure the accuracy of the information provided, the author and publisher assume no responsibility for errors or omissions.

The advice and strategies contained herein may not be suitable for every situation. This book is sold with the understanding that the author is not engaged in rendering legal, accounting, or other professional services. If professional assistance is required, the services of a competent professional person should be sought.

Dedication

This book is dedicated to my amazing wife, Tracy. Thank you my love for finding me and loving me with all of your heart. I am truly blessed and so grateful to be yours.

This book is also dedicated to incredibly talented clients from around the world. This is for the coaches, creatives, entrepreneurs, leaders, and visionaries who inspire me every single day with your gifts, your wisdom, and your courage.

You remind me, again and again, that brilliance comes in many forms - and that the world is richer when people are willing to be seen for who they truly are.

This book is for all of you. And it's also for those of you who are standing at the edge of discovering your own Expert Authority - feeling the pull to step forward, speak up, and finally claim the space you've earned.

May these pages remind you of what I already know to be true:

You are capable.
You are worthy.
And your voice matters.

Table of Contents

Introduction: Why Expert Authority Changes Everything (And Why Talent Alone Isn't Enough)

Chapter 1: The Expert Authority Gap

Chapter 2: Busy, Visible, and Still Overlooked: Why Visibility Without Authority Is a Trap

Chapter 3: Busting Out of Imposter Syndrome and Deciding to Become the Authority

Chapter 4: Pick a Lane (and Own It): Defining Your Authority Zone

Chapter 5: How to Rewire Your Subconscious So You Can Show Up Authentically

Chapter 6: Camera-Ready Authority: Deciding to Be Seen Without Freaking Out

Chapter 7: Keep It Simple: The Pros and Cons of Being Multi-Talented

Chapter 8: Why Marketing Your Expert Authority Can Sometimes Feel Awful

Chapter 9: Fear Is a Mothafluffer

Chapter 10: The Expert Authority Code. What It Truly Is - And Why It Works

Chapter 11: C Is for Clarity

Chapter 12: O Is for Ownership

Chapter 13: D Is For Delivery

Chapter 14: E Is For Elevation

Chapter 15: Make Them Quote You. Becoming Memorable, Referable, and In-Demand

Chapter 16: Proof Beats Persuasion. Showcasing Your Expert Authority Without Bragging

Chapter 17: Get Paid for What You Know. Monetizing Your Expert Authority

Chapter 18: From Scattered to Scalable. Packaging Expertise Into Aligned Offers

Chapter 19: Authority Is a Long Game (And That's Your Advantage)

Chapter 20: Living the Expert Authority Code

Chapter 21: An Invitation to Go Further and Mastering Your Expert Authority

Chapter 22: Your Expert Authority Toolkit. Resources I Use and Highly Recommend

Final Chapter: This Is Where It Begins

Introduction: Why Expert Authority Changes Everything (And Why Talent Alone Isn't Enough)

Let me guess.

You're really good at what you do.

You've put in the years. You've taken the courses. You've worked with clients. You've helped people get real results. And yet, when it comes to being seen, recognized, or paid accordingly, something still feels off.

You know you're capable of more - more impact, more income, more opportunities - but it hasn't quite clicked yet.

If that sounds familiar, you're in exactly the right place.

Here's the truth most people won't tell you: being talented is no longer enough.

In today's noisy, scroll-happy world, expertise alone does not automatically translate into visibility, trust, or income.

The people getting booked, featured, referred, and paid at higher levels are not always the most qualified or the most experienced. They are the ones who have learned how to position themselves as an authority.

And authority does not mean being loud, pushy, salesy, or pretending to be someone you're not. Authority means being recognized as the expert, trusted as the guide, and chosen - consistently.

I know this because for more than 25 years I have worked behind the scenes and on the front lines of media, branding, broadcasting, and personal brand strategy. I've built podcasts, launched brands, produced a ton of content, and helped experts step into the spotlight with confidence and credibility.

Over the years, I have coached and guided thousands of entrepreneurs, coaches, authors, speakers, and thought leaders from around the world who were exceptional at what they did, yet struggled to be seen, heard, or paid at the level they deserved.

And I kept seeing the same pattern play out again and again.

Brilliant people staying invisible.
Talented experts undercharging.
Passionate professionals burning out chasing attention instead of building authority.

That's exactly why I created **The Expert Authority Code.**

The code is not about hustling harder, posting more, or becoming famous. It is about understanding how authority actually works - and how to build it in a way that feels aligned, ethical, sustainable, and profitable.

Inside these pages, you are about to embark on a powerful journey. A journey that will help you stop blending in, stop second-guessing yourself, and stop waiting for permission to be seen as the expert you already are.

You will learn how to position your experience, your voice, and your value so the right people recognize you, trust you, and want to work with you.

Authority changes everything.

And once you understand the Expert Authority Code, you will never approach your business - or your brilliance - the same way again.

If at any point you want deeper guidance, hands-on support, or to go beyond what this book offers, I invite you to visit <u>ExpertAuthorityCoach.com</u>, where you'll find resources, programs, and opportunities to work with me directly.

I've helped hundreds of overwhelmed entrepreneurs, coaches, authors and thought leaders from around the world become the go-to authority in their field – and I can do the same for you.

Just head to **ExpertAuthorityCoach.com** and book a FREE chat with me.

You know in your heart that it's time. It's time to stop being overlooked and start being recognized as the Expert Authority you truly are.

So if you're ready to begin, let's move beyond this introduction and begin the work in Chapter 1.

Chapter 1: The Expert Authority Gap

There's a gap no one warns you about when you decide to build a business based on your expertise.

I call it **The Expert Authority Gap**.

It's the space between knowing your stuff and being recognized for it. And this is where most experts get stuck.

I see it every single day.

Over the years, I've coached executives stepping out of corporate roles, keynote speakers ready for bigger stages, business coaches scaling their practices, and authors who had powerful messages but struggled to get traction.

On paper, these are highly capable people. Smart. Experienced. Credible. In many cases, they've been doing their work for decades.

Yet they come to me feeling frustrated, confused, and quite often, discouraged.

They'll say things like,

"I know I'm good at what I do, but I'm not getting the results I expected."

"People love working with me once they find me - I just

don't know why more people aren't finding me."

"I feel like I'm always explaining myself instead of being instantly understood."

Some are coaches who've been in business for years but still feel like they're starting over every single month.

Some are authors, healers, consultants, or creatives who've invested heavily in their growth yet feel invisible online.

Others are multi-passionate experts who can do a lot of things well - but aren't known for one clear thing.

They're not beginners.
They're not unqualified.
And they're definitely not lazy.

What they're missing isn't talent.

It's authority.

The Authority Gap shows up when you're working harder than people who seem less qualified than you. When you're constantly explaining what you do instead of being instantly understood. When you're busy, but not booked at the level you should be.

I've seen this play out with a senior executive I once coached who had led global teams, managed multimillion-dollar budgets, and advised boards at the highest level.

When she transitioned into consulting, she assumed her experience would speak for itself. Instead, she found herself underpricing her services, blending into the noise online, and watching others with far less experience command bigger fees and better opportunities.

Nothing was wrong with her expertise.
But everything was unclear about her authority.

Another client - an accomplished author and speaker - came to me exhausted from trying to be everywhere at once. Social media. Podcasts. Events. Collaborations. He was visible, but not positioned. People liked him, but they didn't quite know why they should hire him over anyone else.

Once we clarified his message, anchored his authority, and aligned his visibility with a clear expert identity, opportunities started showing up without him chasing them. Speaking invitations increased. Sales conversations became easier. His confidence shifted because his positioning finally matched his experience.

That's what closing the Authority Gap looks like.

Most people assume the solution is more exposure.
More posts.

More platforms.
More hustle.

But effort isn't the issue.

Positioning is.

Authority is not built by accident, and it is not built by volume. It's built through clarity, consistency, and credibility - strategically expressed.

The experts who close the Authority Gap understand something critical: people don't buy the best expert.

They buy the clearest one.

When authority is in place, everything changes. Marketing feels lighter. Sales feel more natural. Opportunities start finding you. You stop chasing, convincing, and proving.

The Authority Gap is not a failure.

It's feedback.

And once you understand how to close it, you don't just get seen.

You get chosen.

Authority Gap Diagnostic: Where Are You Getting Stuck?

Before we go any further, I want you to pause and take an honest look at where you are right now.

This is not a test that you pass or fail.
It's a mirror.

Read each statement and notice what lands. The more statements you recognize yourself in, the wider your Authority Gap may be.

Answer yes or no to each statement:

1. People often say, "You do so many things" or ask you to explain what you do - even after you've already explained it.

2. You get great results for clients, but referrals and opportunities are inconsistent.

3. You feel confident in your work, but hesitant when it comes to visibility, pricing, or self-promotion.

4. You spend time creating content, yet it doesn't consistently lead to inquiries or sales.

5. You know you're experienced, but you still compare yourself to others who seem less qualified yet more visible.

6. You feel busy and productive, but not recognized at the level you expected by now.

7. You've invested in courses, coaches, or certifications, yet something still feels missing.

8. You sometimes downplay your experience to avoid sounding "too much" or "too salesy."

9. You attract the wrong clients - or clients who question your value or pricing.

10. You secretly feel frustrated because you know you have more to offer than your current results reflect.

Your Results

- **0 to 2 yes answers**
  Your Authority Gap is likely small, but refinement and clarity will unlock your next level.

- **3 to 6 yes answers**
  You have solid expertise, but your authority is not being clearly or consistently expressed. This is where most capable experts sit.

- **7 or more yes answers**
  Your Authority Gap is actively limiting your visibility, income, and opportunities - even though your expertise is strong.

An Important Reframe

If you saw yourself in this list, take this in:

Your gap is not a confidence problem.

It's not a motivation problem.

And it's not because you're behind.

It simply means your experience has outgrown your positioning.

And that's good news.

Because authority is learnable, buildable, and entirely within your control.

In the next chapter, we're going to break down exactly why expertise alone doesn't create authority - and what actually does.

Turn the page when you're ready.

Chapter 2: Busy, Visible, and Still Overlooked: Why Visibility Without Authority Is a Trap

If I had a dollar for every time someone told me,"I just need more visibility,"
I'd probably be writing this book from a ritzy beach resort somewhere - umbrella drink included.

Here's what most experts don't realize until they're already exhausted:

Visibility without authority is one of the fastest paths to burnout.

Posting more.
Showing up everywhere.
Saying yes to everything.
Trying to be louder in an already noisy world.

It looks productive. It feels productive.

But it doesn't always move the needle - especially when your authority isn't in place first.

I see this pattern every single day in my work.

Talented, passionate people come to me doing meaningful, life-changing work, yet they're stuck in business models that keep them small, time-poor, and under-recognized. They're visible enough to stay busy, but not positioned strongly enough to scale, expand, or truly lead in their space.

They're running hard, but they're not moving forward in the way they expected.

Let me show you exactly what I mean.

Julia's Story: Brilliant, Successful… and Invisible to the World

When Julia Loggins first came to me, she already had what most people would call a successful business.

She was a highly experienced colon hydrotherapist in Santa Barbara, California, and had been doing this work for decades. Her clients loved her. She got real results. Her practice stayed consistently busy.

From the outside, everything looked great.

But here was the reality:

Only a small group of people knew about her.
Her work was incredibly time-intensive.

And the impact of what she offered was limited by geography and the number of hours in a day.

Julia wasn't struggling - but she was capped.

And that distinction matters.

So many experts assume that if they're making money and helping people, that's as good as it gets. They don't pause long enough to ask the bigger, more expansive question:

What if this work was meant to reach far more people than just those who can physically show up?

When I looked at Julia's business, I didn't see a local service.

I saw an international gut health expert hiding in plain sight.

What she had wasn't just a practice.
It was intellectual property.
It was education.
It was transformation.
It was authority waiting to be claimed.

The first thing we worked on wasn't social media.
It wasn't products.
And it wasn't visibility.

It was identity.

Julia, like so many experts, saw herself as someone who does the work, not someone who leads the conversation. She hadn't fully owned the depth, importance, and scale of what she knew.

Together, we clarified her authority position, refined her messaging, expanded her vision, and helped her confidently step into the role of expert - not just practitioner.

Once authority was established, visibility became powerful instead of draining.

Today, Julia Loggins is:
An internationally recognized gut health expert
A best-selling author
The creator of multiple gut health supplement products
And a TikTok influencer with tens of thousands of raving fans

Same woman.
Same knowledge.
Same heart.

What changed was her Expert Authority.

Want to see for yourself?

You can visit her website at DareToDetoxify.com

Barbara's Story: Authority Has No Age Limit

Now let me introduce you to Barbara Savin.

Barbara is a master Reiki healer and hypnotherapist with over 40 years of experience. When I met her, she was working out of the Four Seasons in Westlake Village, California. She had a small group of private clients there, along with a few celebrity clients she worked with quietly and discreetly.

Her work was powerful.
Her reputation was solid.
And very few people knew about her.

Like many healers, Barbara's work was deeply time-intensive. She traveled to clients' homes or met them in her office. Her impact was limited by time, location, and physical presence.

But Barbara had a dream she couldn't let go of.

She told me she had always wanted to create a podcast - a space to share her stories, her wisdom, and the gift of healing with people all over the world. She wanted others to experience healing modalities, even if they never booked a private session.

There was just one problem.

At her age she was convinced she wouldn't be able to figure out all of the technology needed to produce a podcast.

The idea of recording, editing, publishing, and marketing a podcast felt overwhelming - even impossible.

What Barbara needed wasn't more visibility.

She needed belief - and a framework that made authority feel accessible and achievable.

Step by step, I guided her through the process. We worked through the technophobia, simplified the systems, and reframed authority as leadership, not perfection.

And here's what happened.

Barbara became a bona fide podcaster.

Today, she:
Reaches audiences all around the world
Has published over 140 episodes of The Spiritual Warrior Coach Podcast

Has interviewed rock and roll legend Pat Benatar
And has done all of this at the ripe young age of 77

Let that sink in.

Don't believe me?

You can visit her website at **BarbaraSavin.com**

The Pattern You Need to See

Julia and Barbara work in very different fields.
They're at different stages of life.
And their paths look nothing alike.

But the pattern is identical.

Both were:
Highly skilled and deeply experienced
Respected by a small circle
Trapped in time-based, location-based business models
And underestimating the true scale of their authority

Once authority came first, visibility became a multiplier, not a drain.

And this is the truth I want you to walk away with:

More visibility is not the answer if authority isn't clear.

Visibility amplifies whatever is already there.
If authority is unclear, visibility amplifies confusion.
If authority is clear, visibility amplifies trust.

That's the difference between being busy and being in demand.

What Comes Next

Here's the moral of the story - and it matters more than you think:

It's never too late.
Not to pivot.
Not to expand.
Not to learn something new.
And not to become the expert authority you were always meant to be.

Authority is not about age, tech skills, or perfection.
It's about making a decision.

And that's exactly what we'll talk about in the next chapter.

Because before strategies work…
Before visibility sticks…
Before opportunities start finding you…

You must decide to **be** the authority.

And once that decision is made, everything else begins to fall into place.

Authority Trap Checklist: Are You Visible or Are You Leading?

Before you move on, I want you to pause and check in with yourself.

This is not about judgment.
It's about awareness.

Read each statement and notice what resonates. If you answer yes to several of these, you may be caught in the visibility trap - showing up a lot without being positioned as the authority.

Answer yes or no to each statement:

1. You create content consistently, but it rarely leads to clear inquiries or opportunities.

2. You feel pressure to be everywhere online just to stay relevant.

3. You say yes to podcasts, collaborations, or projects that don't truly align with your expertise.

4. You spend a lot of time educating for free, but struggle to convert that visibility into income.

5. People compliment your work, yet still ask basic questions about what you do or who you help.

6. You feel busy and visible, but not fully respected or recognized as a leader in your space.

7. You hesitate to narrow your message because you don't want to leave anyone out.

8. You rely on platforms or algorithms instead of a clear authority position to drive opportunities.

9. You've increased your visibility, but your pricing, confidence, or demand hasn't increased with it.

10. You secretly feel tired of "showing up" without seeing the return you expected.

Your Results

- **0 to 2 yes answers**
  Your visibility is likely aligned with authority. A few refinements will strengthen your leadership position.

- **3 to 6 yes answers**
  You have strong expertise, but your visibility may

be outpacing your authority. This is where recalibration creates breakthroughs.

- **7 or more yes answers**
  You are likely stuck in the visibility trap. You are working harder than necessary without being positioned as the expert authority.

An Important Truth to Remember

If you recognized yourself in this checklist, take this in:

The problem is not that you're showing up too much. The problem is that you're showing up without a clear authority foundation.

Visibility is a tool.
Authority is the strategy.

And when those two are aligned, everything changes.

In the next chapter, we're going to explore the mindset shift that must happen before authority can truly take root - the decision to stop waiting for permission and start leading with intention.

Turn the page when you're ready.

Chapter 3: Busting Out of Imposter Syndrome and Deciding to Become the Authority

Before we talk about strategy…
Before visibility works…
Before opportunities start showing up…

There's a decision that must be made.

And it has nothing to do with your website, your logo, or how many followers you have.

Authority starts with identity.

Not tactics.
Not tools.
Not trends.

Identity.

Every expert I've ever worked with hits this moment - whether they realize it or not. It's the moment where you stop asking for permission and start owning what you already know.

And here's where many people hesitate.

Because stepping into authority often brings up something uncomfortable, sneaky, and very common:

Imposter syndrome.

Let's Talk About Imposter Syndrome (Because You're Not Broken)

Imposter syndrome is the persistent belief that you're not as capable, qualified, or deserving as others think you are - and that sooner or later, someone is going to "figure you out."

In other words:

• Who am I to say this?
• There are people who know more than me.
• I need one more certification before I put myself out there.
• Once I feel more confident, then I'll step up.

Sound familiar?

Here's the irony:

Imposter syndrome shows up most often in high achievers.

The people who care deeply about doing good work.
The people who have integrity.
The people who understand nuance, responsibility, and impact.

In fact, the more you know, the more aware you are of what you don't know - and that awareness can easily turn into self-doubt if you're not careful.

Meanwhile, the loudest voices in the room often have the least depth.
(Yes - that part is still true.)

What Actually Creates Imposter Syndrome

Imposter syndrome doesn't come from lack of skill.
It comes from a few very specific places:

Comparison.
Looking sideways instead of inward. Measuring yourself against someone else's highlight reel.

Perfectionism.
Believing authority requires flawlessness. It doesn't. It requires leadership.

Early conditioning.
Many of us were taught not to brag, not to be "too much," and not to put ourselves forward.

Waiting for permission.
From peers. From the industry. From some imaginary panel of experts who never actually meet.

Here's the truth I tell my clients - and I want you to hear it clearly:

Confidence is not a prerequisite for authority.
Authority is what creates confidence.

Authority Is Not Arrogance (Let's Clear That Up)

One of the biggest mindset blocks I see - especially with thoughtful, heart-centered experts - is the fear of appearing arrogant.

So let me reframe this for you.

Authority is not saying, "I know everything."
Authority is saying, "I know enough to guide someone who is a few steps behind me."

Authority is not ego.
It's service.

When you withhold your voice because you don't feel "ready," the people who need your guidance don't get it.

And that's not humility.

That's hesitation.

The Identity Shift That Changes Everything

At some point, every expert has to move from this identity:

"I help people."

To this one:

"I lead people."

That doesn't mean you stop learning.
It doesn't mean you stop growing.
It means you stop shrinking.

Deciding to be the authority is an internal shift first. It's the moment you say:

- I don't need to know everything to be valuable
- My experience counts
- My voice matters
- And my work deserves to be seen

This is where imposter syndrome begins to lose its grip.

Not because it disappears - but because it no longer gets to drive.

An Exercise That Changes Everything: Take the Focus Off You

This is one of the most powerful shifts I teach my clients - and it's deceptively simple.

Imposter syndrome thrives when the focus is on you.

How you look.
How you sound.
What people will think.
How you'll be perceived.

So let's flip that.

The Authority Reframe Exercise

Ask yourself these questions - and answer them honestly:

- Who am I here to help?
- What problem am I uniquely positioned to solve?
- What relief, clarity, or transformation can I offer?

Now here's the key question:

What happens if I don't show up?

Because when imposter syndrome wins:

- Someone stays stuck
- Someone doesn't get the answer you hold
- Someone doesn't feel seen, supported, or guided

When you shift the focus from *How will I be perceived?*
to *Who needs what I know?*
everything changes.

Authority isn't about spotlighting yourself.
It's about showing up in service.

And when your intention is service, confidence has room
to grow.

How High-Level Experts Work With Imposter Syndrome

Here's something no one tells you:

Imposter syndrome doesn't go away at the top.

The difference is that established authorities don't obey it.

They recognize it as a sign of growth.
They don't wait to feel ready.
They move forward with the discomfort.

They understand this simple truth:

You don't become the authority after you feel confident.
You feel confident after you decide to lead.

The Decision Point

Here's the moment that matters most.

You don't wake up one day and magically feel like the authority.

You decide to be the authority - and your actions begin to follow.

That decision changes how you speak.
How you show up.
How others perceive you.
And eventually, how you see yourself.

In the next chapter, we'll talk about how to define your Authority Zone - the one clear lane where your expertise, experience, and impact intersect.

Because once you decide to be the authority, the next step is making sure the world knows exactly what you're the authority in.

And trust me - that clarity is where momentum really starts.

Here Are Your Daily Authority Mantras

I trust my experience. I lead with clarity. I claim my authority.
My voice matters. My work serves. I show up with authority.
I no longer wait for permission. I lead from who I am.
I don't need to know everything. I know enough to lead.
I am safe to be seen. I am ready to lead.

Chapter 4: Pick a Lane (and Own It): Defining Your Authority Zone

Once you decide to be the authority, the next question becomes:

Authority in what?

Because here's the truth - and this one can sting a little:

If you're not crystal clear about what you're known for, neither is anyone else.

This is where many experts unintentionally sabotage their own success. They're talented, capable, and passionate... but their message is scattered. They're known for many things, instead of one clear thing.

And clarity is the currency of authority.

What Is Your Authority Zone?

Your Authority Zone is the sweet spot where three things intersect:

- Expertise - what you know

- Experience - what you've lived, navigated, and learned
- Results - what you've helped create for yourself or others

This is not about listing every skill you have. It's about identifying the work you're best positioned to lead.

Your Authority Zone answers three essential questions:

- Who do I help?
- What do I help them do?
- Why does it matter?

If any one of these is fuzzy, your authority becomes fuzzy too.

Why Being "Multi-Passionate" Can Dilute Authority

I work with a lot of multi-talented, multi-passionate people. And if that's you, let me say this first: there is nothing wrong with you.

But there is a problem when your audience can't immediately understand how you help them.

Authority doesn't mean you only are one thing. It means you're known for one thing.

You can have layers, depth, and evolution - but the doorway into your world must be clear.

Think of it this way: People don't hire "versatile." They hire relevant.

The Stapler vs. Sandwich Problem

This is one of my favorite analogies, because it makes people laugh - and then it makes them pause.

Many entrepreneurs, coaches, and service providers are out there selling a stapler.

And not just any stapler - the best stapler in the world.

This stapler has all the bells and whistles. It comes in multiple colors. It's on sale this month for 50% off. And you're convinced everyone needs it.

So you're posting about the stapler.

Emailing about the stapler.

Launching the stapler.

But here's the problem: your potential clients don't want a stapler. They just want a sandwich.

They're hungry. They're overwhelmed. They're tired. They need relief, clarity, support, or a solution right now.

And while you're passionately selling the stapler, they're thinking: "This sounds nice… but it's not what I need."

This is where authority breaks down.

Because authority is not about pushing what you think people should buy. It's about understanding what they actually need - and meeting them there.

Authority Is Client-Centered, Not Offer-Centered

This is something I drill into my clients again and again: your audience does not care about your program. They care about their problem.

Your Authority Zone isn't defined by what you want to sell. It's defined by what your people need help with - and what you are uniquely equipped to help them solve.

When you're clear on that, your offers evolve naturally.

Sometimes that means repositioning a program, renaming an offer, or realizing the "stapler" is actually a next step - not the entry point.

Authority requires empathy. It requires listening. And it requires being willing to pivot.

Clarifying Who You Help (And Who You Don't)

One of the most powerful authority moves you can make is narrowing your focus.

Not everyone is your client. And that's a good thing.

When you try to help everyone, no one feels fully seen.

Clarity sounds like:

- "I help overwhelmed entrepreneurs simplify their message."
- "I help experts turn their knowledge into visibility and income."
- "I help people move from invisible to in-demand."

Notice how those statements make someone either lean in… or realize it's not for them. That's authority.

What You Help Them Do (The Transformation)

Authority lives in outcomes, not features.

People don't want coaching sessions, programs, or tools. They want confidence, clarity, relief, momentum, and results.

Your Authority Zone should clearly articulate the transformation you help create.

Before → After.

Confused → Clear. Invisible → Recognized. Overwhelmed → Focused.

That's what people remember.

Why It Matters (This Is Where Authority Deepens)

The "why" is what turns expertise into leadership.

Why does this work matter? Why now? Why does it change lives?

When you connect your work to a bigger purpose, authority deepens - for you and your audience.

People don't just buy solutions. They buy meaning.

Becoming Known for One Clear Thing

Let me say this gently - and clearly: you don't lose opportunities by being specific. You gain them.

When you're known for one clear thing, referrals become easier, messaging becomes simpler, confidence increases, and opportunities align faster.

Your Authority Zone is not a box. It's a foundation.

From there, you can expand, evolve, and grow - without confusing your audience.

What Comes Next

Now that you've decided to be the authority and you're defining your Authority Zone, the next step is learning how to communicate it clearly and powerfully.

In the next chapter, we'll dive into Authority Messaging - how to speak in a way that makes people instantly understand your value, trust your voice, and remember you.

Because once your Authority Zone is clear, your message should do the heavy lifting — not you.

Authority Zone Exercise: Find Your Sweet Spot (Without Overthinking It)

This is one of those exercises that looks simple on the surface - and then creates big "aha" moments if you actually do it.

So promise me something before you start: don't try to be clever. Don't try to be impressive. And definitely don't try to sound like someone else.

This is about clarity - not perfection.

Step 1: Start With What You Know (Expertise)

Grab a piece of paper and answer this: What do people already come to you for help with?

Not what you wish they came to you for. Not what you want to sell them next month. What they already ask you about.

Look for patterns: questions you answer repeatedly, advice people thank you for, topics you could talk about all day. Write it down exactly as it shows up in real life.

Step 2: Layer in What You've Lived (Experience)

Now ask yourself: What have I personally navigated, overcome, or deeply experienced?

This might include career pivots, burnout, reinvention, healing, visibility struggles, or starting over (more than once).

Your lived experience matters more than you think. This is where your authority becomes relatable - not theoretical.

Step 3: Anchor It in Results (Proof)

Next question: What results have I helped create - for myself or for others?

These don't have to be flashy or famous. Results look like confidence, clarity, relief, momentum, sustainable growth, or someone finally feeling seen.

Authority is built on outcomes - not titles.

Step 4: Answer the Big Three (This Is the Core)

Using what you wrote above, complete these sentences:

- I help _______________________________
- to ___________________________________

- so that ________________________________

If you need three paragraphs to explain it, you're not there yet.

Step 5: The Stapler vs. Sandwich Check

Ask yourself honestly: Am I selling a stapler... when my people actually need a sandwich?

Is what you're promoting solving their most urgent problem - or are you pushing an offer you're excited about without meeting them where they are?

If there's a mismatch, this is your pivot point. Authority means recognizing the hunger - and offering the sandwich first. You can always introduce the stapler later.

Step 6: The "Known For" Test

Finally, ask: If someone were to recommend me to a friend, what would they say I'm known for?

If that answer feels vague, scattered, or inconsistent - that's your signal. Your Authority Zone should make that sentence easy to finish.

Final Reminder

Your Authority Zone is not about boxing yourself in. It's about giving people a clear doorway into your world.

Once they understand why you matter and how you help, everything becomes easier: your messaging, your offers, your confidence, your visibility.

Clarity creates confidence. And confidence creates authority.

Chapter 5: How to Rewire Your Subconscious So You Can Show Up Authentically

After more than two decades of working with business owners, coaches, authors, executives, speakers, and visionaries, I can tell you this with certainty:

The people who struggle the most with visibility, pricing, and authority are not underqualified.
They are over-capable - and their subconscious knows it.

You want to be seen.
You want to step into your authority and charge what you're worth.

And yet, every time you go to raise your hand, post the video, pitch yourself, get on stage, or increase your prices, something in your body quietly says no.

That moment is often labelled as **imposter syndrome**.

But here's the twist most people miss:

That response is not self-doubt.
It's not sabotage.
And it's certainly not a character flaw.

It's your subconscious doing exactly what it was designed to do - keep you safe.

Your subconscious mind is brilliant.

It runs on patterns, protection, and past experience. Long before you became a business owner, speaker, or leader, it learned very specific rules about what happens when you stand out, speak up, or are seen.

If, at any point in your life, visibility led to rejection, embarrassment, criticism, or loss of belonging, your subconscious took notes.

Its job is not to help you grow.
Its job is to help you survive.

When you understand how the subconscious actually works - and give it new, safer options - you stop fighting yourself.

You stop forcing confidence.
You stop pushing through resistance.
And you start showing up calmer, clearer, and far more magnetic.

Let me show you how.

1. Understand Where Real Change Happens (Hint: It's Not in Your Thinking)

Your conscious mind is fantastic at strategy.

It plans launches, builds offers, sets goals, and makes logical decisions.

But the part of you that whispers, "Who do you think you are?"
The part that tightens your chest before you hit "post"?
The part that hesitates just as you're about to raise your price?

That lives in the subconscious.

You cannot logic your way out of a nervous system response.

The subconscious does not respond to arguments or affirmations shouted over fear.
It responds to feelings, repetition, and safety.

So instead of trying to positive-think your way through imposter syndrome, try this:

When resistance shows up, stop arguing with it.
Pause.
Name what's actually happening in your body - fear, shame, vulnerability, exposure.

Treat that sensation as information, not a verdict.

Your body is communicating, not condemning you.

---

2. Let the Root Reveal Itself (Instead of Guessing What's Wrong With You)

One of the biggest mistakes I see business owners make is trying to figure themselves out intellectually.

True subconscious work doesn't come from guessing.
It comes from listening.

When the subconscious is gently accessed through hypnosis, guided recall, journaling, or deep reflection, it will show you exactly where the pattern began.

Often it's not dramatic.
It's meaningful.

- A moment of public embarrassment
- A time you were dismissed or ignored
- A family dynamic where visibility felt unsafe

Those moments didn't mean you weren't capable.

They created survival strategies.

And survival strategies are not flaws.
They are evidence of resilience.

At some point, those strategies kept you safe.
Now, they may be keeping you small.

The work is not to shame them.
The work is to update them.

---

3. The Two Core Wounds I See Blocking Authority (Especially for Women in Business)

While subconscious patterns are deeply personal, two themes appear again and again in my work.

Fear of abandonment

Often expressed as hyper-independence - "I'll just do it myself."

This shows up as overworking, under-receiving, difficulty delegating, and struggling to be supported or seen.

"I'm not enough"

This is deeply tied to rejection. Biologically, exclusion once meant danger.
So even today, visibility can feel threatening - even when success is available.

Neither of these means you lack confidence.
Neither of these means you are broken.

They simply mean your nervous system learned how to protect you early on.

Once you stop treating these patterns as truths and start seeing them as adaptations, change becomes possible - and sustainable.

---

4. Regulate Your Nervous System Before Any Visibility Moment

Visibility fails when the body is dysregulated.

That's why no branding strategy works if your nervous system feels unsafe.

Before you speak, post, record, pitch, or promote, try this simple 2 to 5 minute reset:

- Place one hand on your heart
- Take three slow, deep breaths
- Recall one genuine moment of joy, connection, or ease from the last 24 hours
- Stay with that felt experience for 20 to 30 seconds

Then speak or record while that sensation is still present.

Your message doesn't just land through words.
It lands through state.

People feel authenticity before they understand it.

---

5. Rewire the Subconscious Through Repetition and Safety

This is where real transformation accelerates.

The subconscious loves repetition.
And it is especially receptive right before sleep.

You don't need to be hypnotizable.
You need consistency.

Try this practice:

- Record a short, calming audio with one new truth

    - "I am safe when I am visible."

    - "My voice creates connection."
        - Listen nightly before sleep
        - Pair it with a physical cue - hand on heart, a scent, a relaxed posture

This links visibility with safety in the body.

Over time, the subconscious begins to relax its grip.

That's not woo.
That's neuroscience.

---

6. Use Mirror and Energy Awareness to Find Where You're Still Hiding

Your brand can only be as clear as your inner alignment.

If parts of you are hidden, your message will feel diluted or confusing to others.

Try this simple mirror practice:

Stand in front of a mirror.
Say one clear truth about your work out loud:

"I help ___ do ___."

Notice what happens in your body.

Tightness?
Avoidance?
A story that pops up?

Don't judge it.
Breathe into it.

This is how you stop being a chameleon trying to fit in - and start becoming a beacon for the people who need you.

7. Take Small Visibility Actions That Prove You're Safe

The subconscious doesn't trust promises.
It trusts evidence.
You don't need a giant leap.
You need calibrated exposure.

Try one of these:

- Post a short, unscripted video after regulating your nervous system
- Raise one price slightly and notice what feelings arise
- Ask for feedback from a safe, supportive circle

Each small success sends new data to your subconscious:

Visibility does not equal danger.
Authenticity does not equal rejection.

That's how imposter syndrome dissolves - not through force, but through proof.

A Gentle Reminder Before You Move On

Your subconscious learned its patterns to keep you alive.
It is not your enemy.
It is your most loyal protector.

Your role now is to offer it new experiences of safety -
gently, consistently, and with compassion.

This is how you stop playing small by accident
and start leading with authority by design.

Show up as you are. That's who your people have been
waiting for.

Chapter 6: Camera-Ready Authority: Deciding to Be Seen Without Freaking Out

Before strategies work.
Before visibility compounds.
Before opportunities begin to find you.

There is a decision that must be made.

Authority is not something you earn after you feel confident.
Authority begins the moment you decide to lead.

Not because you have another credential.
Not because you finally feel ready.
But because someone needs what you know now.

This is where many capable experts hesitate.

They wait to feel confident.
They wait to feel polished.
They wait to feel certain.

And while they wait, quieter voices with less depth step forward.

Authority Is a Decision, Not a Credential

One of the biggest misconceptions I see is the belief that authority comes from permission.

Permission from an industry.
Permission from peers.
Permission from an invisible panel of experts who never actually meet.

Real authority does not come from being chosen.
It comes from choosing yourself.

When you decide to be the authority, your posture changes.
Your voice steadies.
Your presence lands differently.

That shift is felt long before it is explained.

Why Confidence Matters More Than You Think

Here's something most people will never say out loud:

Potential clients can feel uncertainty instantly.

They may not be able to name it, but they sense it in your tone, your pacing, your body language, and your hesitation. When confidence is missing, people subconsciously wonder:

Can I trust this person to guide me?
Do they believe in what they're offering?
Will they stand firm when things get uncomfortable?

This is not about being perfect.
It's about being grounded.

Confidence communicates safety.
And safety is what people are buying.

When confidence is absent, people hesitate. When confidence is embodied, people lean in.

Confidence Is Service, Not Ego

Many thoughtful, heart-centered experts hold back because they fear appearing arrogant.

So let me say this clearly:

Confidence is not ego.
Confidence is responsibility.

If you know you can help someone, withholding your voice does not make you humble. It makes your work harder to find.

Confidence says, "I am willing to be seen so someone else can move forward."

That is service.

Why On-Camera Confidence Is an Authority Accelerator

Video collapses trust timelines.

People can hear your voice.
They can feel your energy.
They can decide quickly whether you are someone they want to learn from or work with.

And the good news is this:

You do not need to be young.
You do not need to be slick.
You do not need to be perfect.

You need to be present, clear, and consistent.

When you shift your focus from "How do I look?" to "How does this help someone?" your nervous system relaxes. Your delivery improves. Your authority comes through naturally.

The Five Fears That Show Up on Camera (and What to Do Instead)

In my work as an Expert Authority Coach, I see the same fears surface again and again.

"I don't look good on camera."
This fear is fueled by comparison and unrealistic

standards. Improve the conditions with simple lighting and camera placement, then redirect your attention to the person you're serving. People connect with warmth, not perfection.

"Who would want to hear from me?"
This is imposter syndrome in disguise. Someone needs your exact experience and voice. Speak to one person who needs help, not to the crowd.

"I'm too old for this."
Experience is an asset. Wisdom builds trust faster than trends ever will.

"I don't know what to say."
Clarity solves this. One message per video. One promise. Short and focused beats long and scattered.

"People will judge me."
They might. But the people you are here to help will thank you. Focus on them.

Mindset Shifts That Build Real Confidence

Confidence is not positive thinking. It is trained focus.

Shift from self-evaluation to service.
Release perfection in favor of presence.
Speak to your cheerleader, not your critic.

Embrace vulnerability strategically.
Practice brevity and clarity.

These shifts calm the nervous system and allow authority to emerge naturally.

Practical On-Camera Foundations That Support Confidence

You do not need a studio. You need reliability.

Good lighting matters more than an expensive camera.
Eye-level camera placement creates connection.
Clear audio builds credibility faster than visuals.
Simple Zoom settings can dramatically improve how you look.

These are not vanity tools.
They remove distractions so your message leads.

Structure Creates Safety

Confidence grows when you know where you're going.

Use simple frameworks.
One idea per video.
A clear opening promise.
A clear close or next step.

You can record freely and edit later. Editing is not cheating. It is leadership through clarity.

Repurposing Builds Momentum

One piece of content can become many.
Long form becomes short clips.
Short clips become captions.
Captions become conversations.

This reduces pressure and increases reach without
burnout.

If You Are Neurodivergent, Read This

Visibility can feel riskier when you are neurodivergent.
That does not make you less capable. It often makes your
insights more valuable.

Break creation into small steps.
Record in short bursts.
Use editing as support.
Leverage hyperfocus when inspiration hits.
Ask for help where needed.

Your differences are not liabilities. They are leadership
assets.

Before You Hit Record - A Grounded Checklist

Clarify one message.
Set up simple lighting.
Check audio.

Position the camera at eye level.
Remove distractions.
Take one breath.
Speak to one person.

Then press record.

The Decision Point

You do not become confident and then decide to lead.

You decide to lead.
And confidence follows.

Reader Practice: The Authority On-Camera Confidence Reset

Before you move on, pause here.

This practice is not about looking polished or performing well.
It's about teaching your nervous system that **being seen is safe** and **leading is allowed**.

Step 1: Set Your Intention (1 minute)

Before you record anything, say this out loud:

"I am not here to impress. I am here to serve."

Then choose **one person** who needs what you know. Not an audience. One human.

This immediately shifts your body out of self-judgement and into leadership.

Step 2: Record Without Publishing (2–5 minutes)

Open your camera or phone.
Do not plan to post this.

Answer this one prompt:

"One thing I wish more people understood about [your area of expertise] is…"

Speak naturally. Pause if you need to. Ramble if you must.

When you're done, stop recording and **do not rewatch yet**.

Your only job is to prove to your nervous system that you can speak and survive.

Step 3: Reflect, Don't Critique (2 minutes)

Now watch the recording once with a specific lens.

Do not assess how you look.

Instead, ask:

- Did I sound like myself?

- Did my message have value?

- Would this help someone?

If the answer is yes, you are already leading.

The 7-Day On-Camera Authority Challenge

This challenge builds confidence through **small, repeatable wins**.

Day 1: Presence

Record a 60-second video introducing who you help and why you care. Do not post.

Day 2: Clarity

Record a short tip that solves one small problem your audience faces.

Day 3: Voice

Record standing up. Notice how your energy shifts.

Day 4: Simplicity

Record a video with just one sentence of value. That's it.

Day 5: Humanity

Share a brief personal insight, lesson, or mistake that shaped your work.

Day 6: Leadership

Record a message beginning with, *"Here's what I want you to remember…"*

Day 7: Decision

Choose one video from the week and post it publicly - imperfectly.

What This Practice Teaches You

- Confidence is a skill, not a personality trait
- Authority is felt through presence, not polish
- Repetition creates safety
- Service dissolves fear

You do not wait until you feel confident to show up.

You show up - and confidence follows.

When you're ready, turn the page.

In the next chapter, we'll discuss the pros and cons of being multi-talented.

Chapter 7: Keep It Simple: The Pros and Cons of Being Multi-Talented

If you're multi-talented, multi-passionate, and capable of doing many things well, let me say this clearly:

Being multi-talented is a gift.

Many of the most creative, impactful, and intelligent people I know fall into this category. They see patterns others miss. They adapt quickly. They bring depth, nuance, and originality to everything they do.

And yet, being multi-talented is also one of the fastest ways to confuse the very people you are trying to help.

Not because you lack skill.

Not because you lack focus.

But because clarity must come before complexity.

The Real Danger of Being Everything to Everyone

When you have many skills, experiences, and interests, it's tempting to lead with all of them.

You list everything you offer.

You explain every angle of what you do.

You try to show the full picture right away.

But your potential clients are not standing where you are.

They are busy.

They are overwhelmed.

They are scanning quickly for relevance.

And when they can't immediately understand who you help and how you help them, they don't lean in.

They scroll past.

This is where many brilliant, multi-talented people get stuck. They assume that more information will create more trust.

In reality, confusion weakens trust.

When people feel unsure, they pause. When they pause, they don't choose.

Why Simplicity Must Come First (Even If You Have More to Offer)

Here's the key distinction most experts miss:

Simplicity is not about hiding your gifts.

It's about sequencing them.

Your job is not to show everything you can do at once.

Your job is to invite the right people into your world.

Once someone is inside your world, then you can reveal more.

That's when your additional skills become an advantage instead of a liability.

Inside your world, people have context.

They understand your voice.

They trust your leadership.

At that point, your range feels expansive, not confusing.

But before that trust is built, complexity creates friction.

Think of it like a doorway.

If the doorway is cluttered, people hesitate to enter.

If the doorway is clear and inviting, they step inside.

Once they're inside, they're happy to explore all the rooms.

How Confusion Quietly Undermines Authority

Authority depends on orientation.

People need to know where to place you in their mind.

If your message changes constantly, or tries to cover too much ground, people don't know what problem you solve first.

They may admire you.

They may enjoy your content.

They may even follow you for years.

But they won't hire you.

Not because you're not capable - but because you're not clearly positioned.

Remember this:

People don't choose experts they have to figure out.

They choose experts who make clarity easy.

Depth Builds Authority. Scatter Dilutes It.

Simplicity does not mean dumbing yourself down.
It does not mean shrinking your intelligence.

And it does not mean abandoning your other talents.

It means choosing a primary lane.

Depth creates association.

Association creates trust.

Trust creates authority.

When people consistently hear you speak about one clear outcome, something powerful happens:

"Oh, this is who they help."

"This is what they're known for."

"This is why I'd work with them."

Your other gifts don't disappear. They support your authority. They deepen your impact once the relationship has begun.

A Reframe for the Multi-Talented Expert

If part of you resists simplicity because it feels limiting, hear this:

You are not choosing a box.

You are choosing an entry point.

A clear authority message is how people find you.

Once they do, your multi-talented nature becomes a strength they are grateful for - not something they have to decipher.

Many of the most recognized authorities you admire are deeply multi-talented. They simply learned how to lead with one clear promise and let the rest unfold naturally.

A Simple Check-In

Ask yourself:

Can someone understand what I do in under five seconds?

Am I leading with outcomes or with explanations?

Am I trying to show how much I know, or make it easy to trust me?

If these questions feel uncomfortable, that's not failure.

That's feedback.

The One Sentence Authority Filter

This is a tool you can use immediately to bring clarity to your message.

Your One Sentence Authority Statement should answer this:

I help [specific type of person] solve [specific problem] so they can achieve [specific outcome].

That's it.

If your sentence:

Needs multiple explanations

Includes several "ands"

Or tries to cover multiple audiences

It's too broad.

Here are a few examples:

"I help coaches clarify their message so they can become the obvious expert in their field."

"I help professionals build confidence on camera so they can attract aligned opportunities."

"I help entrepreneurs turn their experience into authority so clients can find and trust them."

This sentence is not your entire identity.

It is your doorway.

Once people step through it, you can show them everything else you bring to the table.

Before You Move On

You don't need to be everything to everyone.

You need to be someone unmistakable to the right people.

Clarity brings them into your world.

Your depth keeps them there.

This is where simplicity turns into strategy.

And where your Expert Authority begins to scale with ease.

Chapter 8: Why Marketing Your Expert Authority Can Sometimes Feel Awful

Marketing your Expert Authority can feel like one long, never-ending chore - so much so that you might rather do just about anything else than post another "look at me" update on social media.

I hear this all the time from my clients.

They're overwhelmed.
They're exhausted.
And quietly, they're wondering if they're even cut out for this entrepreneurial life.

If you've ever felt a pit in your stomach before hitting "post," questioned your worth while writing an email, or thought, *Why does this feel so hard for me?* - trust me, you are not alone.

And more importantly, there is nothing wrong with you.

Why Marketing Feels Personal (Even When It Shouldn't)

Here's what no one tells you:

When you're an expert, a coach, or a creative, your work is personal. Your ideas come from your lived experience, your values, your heart. So when you market your programs, services, or offers, it can feel like you're marketing *yourself*.

That's why rejection feels sharper.
That's why silence feels louder.
And that's why comparison cuts deeper.

You're not just selling a product. You're putting your voice, your story, and your identity out into the world.

Of course that feels vulnerable.

But vulnerability does not mean weakness. It means you care.

The Lie That Makes Marketing Miserable

Many people have unconsciously absorbed a damaging belief:

"If I talk about what I do, I'm being selfish, salesy, or annoying."

So they hesitate.
They soften their message.
They downplay their impact.

And marketing starts to feel awful because it's disconnected from truth.

Here's the reframe that changes everything:

Marketing is not about convincing.
Marketing is about **inviting**.

It's about letting the right people know, *"I can help you with this."*

When marketing is aligned, it doesn't drain you.
It energizes you.

The Authenticity Factor

In today's noisy online world, people can sense insincerity instantly. Forced messaging, copied formulas, or showing up out of obligation doesn't just feel exhausting for you - it feels flat to your audience.

Your people don't want a polished version of someone else's strategy.

They want *you*.

Your voice.
Your quirks.
Your lived experience.
Your truth.

This is where what I call **the authenticity factor** comes in.

When you stop performing and start sharing from alignment, marketing stops feeling like a performance and starts feeling like connection.

Imposter Syndrome Loves to Hijack Marketing

One of the biggest barriers I see - especially with women and heart-centered experts - is imposter syndrome.

Those quiet inner scripts that say:

"I'm too old to start this."
"I'm not as polished as she is."
"Who's going to listen to me?"

These thoughts don't show up because you're unqualified. They show up because you're stretching.

Imposter syndrome thrives in moments of visibility.

And marketing is visibility.

The goal is not to eliminate these thoughts, but to stop letting them drive.

How I Work With Clients on This

When someone comes to me and says, "Christine, I feel like a fraud," my job is not to hand them another marketing checklist.

My job is to hold up a mirror.

I've worked with CEOs, authors, nonprofit leaders, healers, creatives, and brand-new coaches. No matter how accomplished they are, the pattern is the same:

They've been trying to contort themselves into who they think they *should* be, instead of showing up as who they *are*.

The turning point comes when we identify their true superpower - the natural strength they've been undervaluing or hiding.

Once they claim it, their message shifts.

From hesitant to grounded.
From apologetic to clear.
From invisible to magnetic.

A Story That Says It All

One of my most inspiring clients is Ruth Wilson, an 82-year-old woman who completely defied expectations.

Ruth was one of the first professional female hot air balloonists in Australia. She survived extraordinary challenges and lived a life filled with courage, adventure, and resilience.

Society might have expected her to quietly fade into retirement.

Instead, she chose visibility.

Today, she's a speaker, author, and podcast guest - thriving, visible, and inspiring people across generations.

Her story is proof that your message does not expire. And your authority does not diminish with age.

The Energy You Radiate Matters More Than the Words

Here's something most people don't realize:

Desperation has a scent.

When your marketing carries an unspoken energy of *please choose me*, potential clients feel it immediately - and they pull back.

But when you radiate steadiness, clarity, and grounded confidence, you don't have to beg for attention.

You attract it.

Authority energy says, *"I know who I help, and I know how I help them."*

That energy builds trust faster than any tactic.

Why Audiences Crave Realness More Than Ever

Marketing culture has shifted.

Perfection no longer wins.
Gloss no longer converts.

Audiences crave relatability, humanity, and truth.

That's why platforms like TikTok exploded. Not because people became less professional, but because they became more real.

If you've been comparing yourself to others online and feeling like you don't measure up, hear this:

The less you try to be perfect, the more magnetic you become.

Collaboration Over Hustle

The old model said: grind harder, do it alone, push through.

That model is broken.

The new paradigm is collaboration, partnership, and community.

When you collaborate, your energy multiplies. Your reach expands. And marketing feels lighter because it's shared.

Authority grows faster in rooms than in silos.

Why I Love Podcasting

One of my favorite tools for aligned marketing is podcasting.

There's something intimate about audio. No visual judgment. No algorithm gymnastics. Just your voice connecting directly with someone who chose to listen.

I've seen clients land dream clients after one meaningful podcast conversation.

Marketing doesn't always need to be loud. Sometimes it just needs to be real.

The Bottom Line

Marketing your Expert Authority doesn't have to feel awful.

When you stop forcing yourself into someone else's mold and start showing up with your story, your voice, and your natural energy, everything changes.

Imposter syndrome loosens its grip.
Your audience leans in.
And the right opportunities begin to find you.

If marketing has ever felt like sticking a fork in your eye, take heart.

There is another way.

And it starts with alignment.

Reader Exercises: Reframing the "Awful" Feeling

Exercise 1: The Marketing Reframe (5 minutes)

Complete this sentence in writing:

"When I market my work, I'm afraid people will think I am _________."

Now rewrite it as truth:

"When I market my work, I am actually offering
__________."

Repeat this before you post or send an email.

Exercise 2: From Selling to Serving

Before creating any marketing content, answer this out loud:

- Who is struggling with this right now?
- What would genuinely help them today?
- How can I say this in my own words?

That's your message.

Exercise 3: The Energy Check

Before you hit "publish," ask:

Am I sharing from clarity or from panic?

If it's panic, pause. Breathe. Re-center.
Marketing done from calm authority always lands better.

Exercise 4: One Aligned Post Challenge

This week, create **one piece of content** where your only goal is to help - not to impress, not to sell.

No metrics.
No overthinking.

Just service.

Notice how it feels.

That feeling is your compass.

When you're ready, turn the page.

Because in the next chapter, we'll talk about how to **build trust and authority without burning yourself out with fear** - and how to let your marketing work *for* you, not against you.

Chapter 9: Fear Is a Mothafluffer

Let's just say it out loud.

Fear is a mothafluffer.

It shows up uninvited.
It messes with your head.
It lies convincingly.
And it has an uncanny ability to appear *right* when you're about to do something meaningful.

If you've been following this book so far and thinking, *Yes, I get it… but I'm still scared*, I want you to know something immediately:

You are not weak.
You are not broken.
And you are definitely not alone.

Fear doesn't show up when you're playing small and staying hidden.
Fear shows up when you're standing at the edge of your next level.

My Own Run-Ins With Fear

People often assume that because I've spent decades in media, broadcasting, and visibility, I must be fearless.

Let me gently burst that bubble.

I've felt fear before hitting record.
Fear before pitching myself.
Fear before launching new offers.
Fear before saying, *"This is what I stand for."*

There were moments early in my career where my hands shook before going live. Times when I questioned whether I had the right to take up space. Moments when I worried I'd be judged, misunderstood, or dismissed.

And yes - moments where I seriously considered staying quieter because it felt safer.

But here's what I've learned, and this is important:

Fear didn't mean I was on the wrong path.
Fear meant I was standing at the edge of my truth.

Why Fear Gets Loud When You're About to Be Seen

Fear is not a sign to stop.

Fear is a biological response designed to keep you familiar, not fulfilled.

Your nervous system does not care about your dreams.
It cares about predictability.

Visibility feels unpredictable.
Leadership feels exposed.
Authority feels risky.

So fear tries to pull you back into the known.

It whispers things like:

- "Who do you think you are?"

- "What if this doesn't work?"

- "What if people judge you?"

- "What if you fail publicly?"

But notice something.

Fear rarely says, *"Don't do this because it's meaningless."*
It says, *"Don't do this because it matters."*

What Fear Is Actually Afraid Of

Here's the reframe that changes everything:

Fear is not afraid of your failure.
Fear is afraid of your expansion.

Because once you step fully into your authority:

- You can't unknow what you know.

- You can't unsee your impact.

- You can't go back to hiding comfortably.

Fear knows that on the other side of visibility is momentum.
And momentum changes lives - including yours.

The Tragedy of Unexpressed Brilliance

This is the part that gets me every time.

I've worked with extraordinary people - coaches, creatives, healers, leaders - who sat on ideas for years because they were scared to be seen.

And the cost wasn't just to them.

It was to the people who never heard their message.
The clients who never found them.
The solutions that never reached the people who needed them most.

Your brilliance doesn't exist in a vacuum.

What you've lived.
What you've learned.
What you've survived and mastered.

It's not just for you.

The world doesn't need more polished perfection.
It needs truth.
It needs lived wisdom.
It needs *you*.

Courage Isn't the Absence of Fear

Let's clear this up once and for all.

Courage is not feeling fearless.

Courage is deciding that fear does not get the final say.

Every confident person you admire has felt fear.
The difference is they didn't obey it.

They moved with it.
They spoke anyway.
They showed up anyway.

And each time they did, fear lost a little power.

A New Relationship With Fear

Instead of trying to get rid of fear, try this:

Acknowledge it.
Thank it for trying to protect you.
And move forward anyway.

You can literally say:
"I hear you. And I'm going to lead anyway."

Fear doesn't need to disappear for you to act.
It just needs to stop being the driver.

On the Other Side of Fear

On the other side of fear is not chaos.

It's clarity.
Connection.
Confidence that grows through action.

It's the moment when someone messages you and says,
"I needed to hear this today."

It's the realization that your voice matters more than your
fear ever did.

It's the quiet knowing that you didn't abandon yourself.

Before You Move On

If you take nothing else from this chapter, take this:

Fear is not a flaw in your system.
It is evidence that you are standing at the edge of your
genius.

And genius does not whisper.

It asks to be expressed.

So if fear is showing up for you right now - good.

It means you're closer than you think.

Turn the page when you're ready.

Because next, we're going to talk about what happens **after** you step through fear - how authority compounds, confidence stabilizes, and your visibility begins to work *with* you instead of against you.

And trust me - that's where things get really good.

Chapter 10: The Expert Authority Code. What It Truly Is - And Why It Works

At its core, **The Expert Authority Code** is the repeatable sequence that turns expertise into trust, trust into visibility, and visibility into opportunity.

It answers the real question your clients are asking:

"How do I stop being overlooked and start being chosen - without becoming someone I'm not?"

The Code is not about hype.
It's not about hacks.
And it's definitely not about being louder.

It's about **alignment first, authority second, visibility last** - in that order.

The CODE Acronym.

C.O.D.E.

Here's the framework I strongly recommend.

C — CLARITY

Know who you are, what you do, and why it matters

Clarity is the foundation of authority.

This is where most experts skip ahead — and pay the price later.

Clarity means:

- Owning your identity as an authority
- Defining your Authority Zone
- Saying one clear thing instead of ten impressive ones
- Being instantly understandable

If people don't "get" you, they can't trust you.

O — OWNERSHIP

Decide to be the authority — before the world confirms it

This is the identity shift.

Ownership means:

- Releasing permission-seeking
- Busting imposter syndrome
- Making peace with fear instead of obeying it
- Claiming your experience as valuable

Authority begins the moment you **stop waiting to be chosen**.

This is where confidence stabilizes — not because fear disappears, but because leadership takes the wheel.

D — DELIVERY

Express your authority in a way people can feel

This is where on-camera confidence, voice, presence, and energy come in.

Delivery means:

- Being seen and heard in ways that feel authentic
- Regulating your nervous system before visibility
- Communicating with clarity instead of performance
- Letting your humanity build trust

People don't just buy what you know — they buy how it *lands*.

E — ELEVATION

Let visibility work for you, not against you

Elevation is strategic visibility — not hustle.

It means:

- Marketing from alignment, not desperation
- Choosing platforms that match your strengths
- Collaborating instead of grinding alone
- Allowing opportunities to find you

This is where my mantra I give to all of my clients fits beautifully:

If you're not seen and heard, you're not hired.

But now it has a system behind it — not pressure.

Why This Works (and Why It's Different)

Most systems push visibility first.

This Code does the opposite.

You don't amplify confusion.
You don't market insecurity.
You don't perform authority.

You **build it**, then you express it.

That's why this is not just a framework — it's a philosophy.

To Sum Up The Expert Authority Code:

The Expert Authority Code is the proven process of turning your expertise into clarity, confidence, and visibility - so you're seen, trusted, and chosen.

The Expert Authority Code shows you how to stop hiding your brilliance and start being recognized as the authority you already are.

The Expert Authority Code is how experts go from invisible to in-demand -without pretending, performing, or playing small.

So if you're ready to ditch your hesitation, release the fear of being seen, and fully embrace the Expert Authority Code right now, let's dive into each section of C.O.D.E. in the next four chapters.

Chapter 11: C Is for Clarity

Clarity is the foundation of authority.

And yet, this is where most business owners stumble - not because they aren't smart, capable, or experienced, but because clarity requires *choice*.

It requires restraint.
It requires ownership.
And it requires the courage to stop hiding behind complexity.

I see this every single day.

Talented experts with years of experience, impressive credentials, and real results come to me frustrated that they're not being seen, trusted, or hired at the level they know they deserve.

When we peel back the layers, the issue is almost never effort.

It's clarity.

Why Clarity Comes Before Everything Else

Here's the hard truth:

If people don't immediately understand who you are,
what you do, and why it matters, they will not stick
around long enough to figure it out.

They won't read the whole page.
They won't watch the full video.
They won't ask clarifying questions.

They'll move on.

This is not because they don't care.
It's because the human brain is wired to conserve energy.

Clarity feels safe.
Confusion feels risky.

And authority only forms when people feel oriented and
secure.

The Biggest Mistake Experts Make

Most experts skip clarity and jump straight to visibility.

They post more.
They try more platforms.
They add more offers.

But visibility without clarity only amplifies confusion.

You don't become more authoritative by being everywhere.

You become authoritative by being **understood**.

This is why some people with far less experience seem to get more traction. They aren't better.

They're clearer.

What Clarity Actually Means

Clarity is not about dumbing yourself down.

It's about distilling your brilliance into something other people can grasp quickly.

True clarity means:

- Owning your identity as an authority
- Clearly defining your Authority Zone
- Saying one clear thing instead of ten impressive ones
- Being instantly understandable

Clarity is the difference between someone thinking, *"Interesting…"* and thinking, *"This is for me."*

Owning Your Identity as an Authority

Many business owners struggle here because they're still waiting for permission.

They describe themselves cautiously.
They soften their language.
They downplay their experience.

But authority does not emerge from modesty disguised as humility.

It emerges from ownership.

Owning your authority does not mean claiming to know everything.
It means being confident about what you *do* know and who you can help.

If you don't clearly claim your role, your audience won't assign it to you.

Defining Your Authority Zone

Your Authority Zone is the intersection of three things:

- What you know deeply

- What you've lived or mastered through experience

- What others consistently seek you out for

Most people describe themselves by listing skills.

Authority is built by leading with outcomes.

When you define your Authority Zone, you stop trying to be relevant to everyone and start becoming essential to the right people.

That focus is magnetic.

Why Saying Less Builds More Trust

Here's the paradox most experts resist:

The more you try to show how much you know, the less people remember you.

When you say ten things, your audience remembers none of them.

When you say one clear thing repeatedly, you become associated with it.

That association is authority.

Clarity is not limiting.
It's liberating.

It gives people a hook to remember you by and a reason to trust you.

Being Instantly Understandable

Instant understanding is one of the most powerful forms of authority.

When someone can explain what you do to another person without stumbling, your clarity is working.

If they have to say, *"Well, it's kind of hard to explain…"* you're losing momentum before the conversation even begins.

Authority travels through other people's mouths.

Clarity makes that possible.

Why Clarity Builds Confidence Too

This part surprises many people.

When you get clear, your confidence increases.

You stop second-guessing what to say.
You stop rambling.
You stop over-explaining.

Clarity calms the nervous system because you know where you stand.

And when *you* feel clear, others feel it too.

A Quick Clarity Check

Ask yourself honestly:

- Can I describe what I do in one sentence without explaining further?

- Do people immediately know who I help?

- Am I leading with outcomes or listing credentials?

- Does my messaging feel focused or scattered?

If any of these feel uncomfortable, that's not a failure.

That's feedback.

Why Clarity Is the First Step in the Code

Clarity comes first because everything else depends on it.

Without clarity:

- Ownership feels shaky

- Delivery feels forced

- Visibility feels exhausting

With clarity:

- Confidence stabilizes

- Messaging sharpens

- Authority compounds

This is why C comes first in C.O.D.E.

Not because it's easy - but because it's essential.

The Clarity Exercise: From Confusing to Compelling

Clarity is not something you think your way into. It's something you *decide*.

This exercise is designed to help you stop over-explaining, stop hiding behind complexity, and start communicating your authority in a way people instantly understand.

Take your time with this. Don't rush it. Simplicity is earned.

Step 1: Strip It Back to the Truth

Answer these questions in writing, without trying to sound impressive:

1. Who do I help?

2. What problem do they come to me for most often?

3. What changes for them after working with me?

Now look at your answers and remove anything that sounds vague, fluffy, or overly technical.

What remains is your raw authority.

Step 2: Create Your One Clear Authority Statement

Use this structure:

I help [a specific type of person] solve [a specific problem] so they can [specific outcome].

That's it.

If you feel the urge to add "and," pause.
Clarity lives on the other side of restraint.

Powerful Examples

- I help coaches turn their expertise into clear authority so they can be seen, trusted, and hired.

- I help business owners stop feeling invisible and become the obvious choice in their industry.

- I help professionals build confidence on camera so their message reaches the people who need it.

- I help experts clarify their message so opportunities come to them instead of the other way around.

- I help multi-talented entrepreneurs focus their brilliance and scale their authority.

If someone can repeat your sentence easily, it's working.

Step 3: Clarify Your Core Offer

Most people confuse their audience because they present *too many options* too soon.

Start with one clear offer.

Use this structure:

I offer [type of offer] that helps [who] achieve [result].

Offer and Service Examples

- I offer a 90-day Authority Accelerator Program that helps experts go from invisible to in-demand.

- I offer private coaching that helps business owners clarify their message and lead with confidence.

- I offer on-camera confidence training for professionals who want to show up powerfully on video.

- I offer strategic brand guidance for experts ready to be recognized as authorities.

- I offer a group program that helps coaches stop overthinking and start being chosen.

If someone immediately knows whether it's for them, you're doing it right.

Step 4: Clarify Your Program, Book, or Signature Method

Your intellectual property should be just as clear as your services.

Use this structure:

[Name] is for [who] who want to [primary outcome].

Program and Book Examples

- *The Expert Authority Code* is for experts who want to be seen, trusted, and paid for what they know.

- *The Authority Accelerator 90 Day Program* is for coaches ready to stop hiding and start leading.

- *From Invisible to In-Demand* is for business owners who want clarity, confidence, and clients.

- *Own Your Voice* is for professionals who want to overcome fear and show up on camera.

- *The Visibility Reset* is for experts who are tired of hustling and ready for aligned growth.

If your title requires explanation, it's not finished yet.

Step 5: The Instant Clarity Test

Say your authority statement, offer, or program description out loud.

Then ask yourself:

- Does this sound grounded?

- Does this feel true?

- Would the right person immediately lean in?

If yes, you're done.
If not, simplify again.

Clarity is not about getting it perfect.
It's about getting it *understandable*.

A Final Reframe Before You Move On

Clarity is not what limits you.

It's what lets people find you.

You can be multi-talented, nuanced, and expansive - **after** someone understands why they should listen to you in the first place.

Clarity opens the door.
Depth keeps them inside.

In the next chapter, we'll move into **O - Ownership**, where clarity becomes commitment and you stop waiting for permission to lead.

Because knowing who you are is powerful.
But standing in it?

That's where authority becomes undeniable.

Chapter 12: O Is for Ownership

The Moment You Stop Waiting and Start Leading

Clarity shows you where you stand.

Ownership is what keeps you there.

This is the part of the Expert Authority Code™ that changes everything - not because it's flashy or visible, but because it's internal, decisive, and permanent.

Ownership is the moment you stop asking, *"Am I allowed?"*
And start saying, *"This is mine to lead."*

No announcement required.
No permission granted.
Just a quiet, unwavering decision.

Why Ownership Is the Missing Link for So Many Experts

Most people assume they're stuck because they need more strategy.

More content ideas.
More confidence.
More marketing tactics.

But what I see again and again is something deeper.

They know who they help.
They know what they do.
They even know it works.

What they haven't done yet is *own it*.

Ownership is not about arrogance.
It's not about claiming superiority.
And it's definitely not about pretending to be fearless.

Ownership is about standing behind your work without apology.

When ownership is missing, people hedge.

They soften their language.
They over-explain.
They discount before being asked.
They stay half-visible so they can retreat if needed.

That hesitation is felt instantly.

Ownership Is an Identity Decision

Ownership doesn't come from being chosen.

It comes from choosing yourself.

This is where many experts stall, because ownership removes the safety net of invisibility. Once you fully own your authority, you can't un-know it. You can't go back to hiding comfortably.

Ownership says:

- I believe in the value of my work.

- I trust my lived experience.

- I am willing to be seen in my leadership.

That decision doesn't make fear disappear.

It simply stops fear from being in charge.

What Ownership Changes Immediately

When someone truly steps into ownership, several things shift at once:

- Their voice steadies

- Their messaging sharpens

- Their boundaries strengthen

- Their pricing aligns

- Their presence feels grounded

They stop performing authority and start embodying it.

People respond to that embodiment.

Ownership creates a sense of safety and certainty that others can feel - even if they can't articulate why.

Why Ownership Is Especially Hard for Marginalized Voices

For many people, ownership isn't just a business decision - it's a personal reckoning.

If you've ever been told to be quieter, smaller, more palatable, or less visible, ownership can feel dangerous.

For LGBTQ+ individuals, women, creatives, and anyone who has learned that standing out came with consequences, ownership often activates old survival patterns.

This isn't weakness.

It's conditioning.

And it can be unlearned.

A Client Story: From Hiding to Leading

I want to share the story of a client I worked with in my **90 Day Authority Accelerator Program**.

He is a gay man with deep wisdom, lived experience, and the kind of insight that can only come from navigating life with awareness, resilience, and compassion.

For years, he played small.

Not because he lacked talent - but because fear told him it was safer to stay in the background. Fear of judgment. Fear of visibility. Fear of success.

He knew he wanted to help others.
He knew he had something meaningful to say.
But he stayed half-hidden, offering support quietly and cautiously.

When we began working together, clarity wasn't the issue.

Ownership was.

Over the course of the program, something shifted.

He stopped minimizing his story.
He stopped waiting to be invited.
He stopped editing himself for comfort.

He claimed his voice.

He began speaking from experience instead of apology.
Leading with wisdom instead of hesitation.
Standing in his truth without shrinking it.

And the results followed.

Not just in visibility or income - but in how he carried himself.

Today, he fully owns his success and his role as a guide for others. His work lands with confidence because it comes from truth. His authority feels natural because it's embodied.

That is ownership.

Ownership Is a Daily Practice

Ownership is not a one-time declaration.

It's a series of small, consistent choices:

- Choosing clear language instead of watered-down messaging

- Holding your prices without justification

- Saying no when something isn't aligned

- Showing up even when fear whispers otherwise

Each choice reinforces your authority.

Each choice builds trust - with others and with yourself.

What Happens When You Don't Own It

When ownership is missing, the cost is subtle but significant.

Opportunities pass quietly.
People underestimate you.
Your work feels heavier than it should.

Not because it isn't valuable - but because it isn't fully claimed.

Ownership is what allows your clarity to move through the world with impact.

Ownership Is an Act of Service

Let me be very clear about this.

Owning your authority is not about you.

It's about the people who need your leadership, your experience, and your voice.

When you hide, they miss out.

Ownership says:
"I am willing to be seen so others can be supported."

That is leadership.

That is authority.

Before we move on, take a breath here.

Because in the next chapter, we'll explore **D – Delivery** - how ownership shows up in your voice, your presence, and how people experience you in real time.

Clarity shows you the path.
Ownership commits you to walking it.

And once you do, there's no going back - only forward.

Chapter 13: D Is For Delivery

How Your Authority Is Experienced in the Real World

Clarity defines your authority.
Ownership commits you to it.

Delivery is where people *experience* it.

This is the stage of the Expert Authority Code where your expertise stops living in your head and starts showing up in tangible, trust-building ways.

Delivery is not about being everywhere all at once. It's about being *intentional*.

Because authority isn't what you say you are.
It's what others experience of you consistently.

Why Delivery Matters More Than You Think

You can be clear.
You can fully own your authority.

But if your delivery is inconsistent, confusing, or invisible, trust erodes.

People decide whether to trust you based on:

- How you communicate

- How you show up

- How easy it is to understand and engage with your
  work

Delivery is the bridge between your inner authority and external recognition.

Your Website Is Often the First Proof Point

Your website is not a brochure.
It's not a résumé.
And it's definitely not a place to hide behind vague language.

Your website messaging should immediately answer:

- Who is this for?

- What problem does this solve?

- Why should I trust this person?

The words you choose matter.

Clear headlines.
Outcome-focused language.
Confident, grounded copy.

This is not about sounding clever.
It's about sounding *certain*.

When someone lands on your website, they should feel oriented, reassured, and invited.

That's authority in action.

Social Proof: Let Others Speak for You

One of the most powerful forms of delivery is **borrowed credibility**.

Rave reviews.
Testimonials.
Client stories.

These are not bragging tools.
They are trust accelerators.

When happy clients describe their transformation in their own words, it removes doubt and shortens decision-making time.

Authority compounds when others validate your work publicly.

Speaking Opportunities: Authority in the Room

Speaking is one of the fastest ways to establish authority - especially in your local community.

Business chambers.
Industry groups.
Community events.
Workshops and panels.

When you stand at the front of the room, you are automatically positioned as a leader.

You don't need a massive stage to make a massive impact.

Authority grows one room at a time.

Blogs and Thought Leadership

Written content is another powerful delivery channel.

Blogs allow you to:

- Demonstrate depth of thinking

- Share perspective

- Educate without selling

When done well, blogging positions you as a thinker, not just a service provider.

Authority is built when people begin quoting your ideas -
not just consuming them.

Social Media as Authority Reinforcement

Social media is not about chasing trends.
It's about reinforcing your message.

Authority-based social content:

- Educates

- Clarifies

- Normalizes challenges

- Shares perspective

It doesn't perform.
It leads.

Consistency matters more than polish.
Presence matters more than perfection.

Podcasting: One of the Most Intimate Forms of Delivery

Podcasting holds a special place in authority building
because it creates connection without distraction.

Podcasting also holds a special place in my heart as I

have hosted and produced several podcasts over the past decade, including The Expert Authority Coach Podcast which can be found on Apple Podcasts, Spotify and YouTube.

As a host, you:

- Lead conversations

- Shape narratives

- Build long-term trust

As a guest, you:

- Borrow audiences

- Share authority

- Expand reach through relationship

I've seen podcasting change lives - including my own.

Podcasting isn't just about creating audio content to promote your Expert Authority.

Over the years, I've written and published **five bestselling books**, many of which were born directly from podcast conversations and audience questions:

- *The Social Media and Branding Survival Guide*

- *Podcastonomics*

- *Podcast Pro*

- *Pod Your Way To Success*

- *Grab That Microphone*

- *Your Amazing Itty Bitty Podcast Book*

Podcasting isn't about fame.
It's about familiarity.

People hire voices they trust.

Joint Ventures and Collaborations

Authority accelerates in collaboration.

Think about the Marvel comic book superheroes.

Captain America alone can do some pretty amazing stuff – but when he joins forces with Wolverine, Hulk and Iron Man it's a whole different story.

Joint ventures, partnerships, and shared projects:

- Expand reach

- Build credibility

- Multiply energy

When respected peers align with you publicly, authority transfers naturally.

You don't have to build alone.

Don't feel the need to just be Captain America by yourself.

Writing and Publishing Books

Books remain one of the strongest authority assets available.

They create permanence.
They create positioning.
They create legacy.

You don't need to write a perfect book.
You need to write a *useful* one.

A book says:
"I've thought deeply about this."
"I can guide you."
"I'm here to lead."

Here's a true story..

When I was a producer and host at a popular radio station – the people who had written a book moved up on my list of potential guests to be interviewed. And if they had a bestseller, even better!

Other Powerful Forms of Delivery

Authority can also be delivered through:

- Online courses and masterclasses

- Workshops and intensives

- Email newsletters

- Video series

- Panels and summits

- Media interviews

- Community leadership roles

Delivery is not limited to one format.

It's about choosing the formats that suit *you* and your audience.

Delivery Is About Alignment, Not Exhaustion

Now remember, you do **not** need to do **all** of this.

You need to do what feels aligned, sustainable, and strategic.

The best delivery system is one you can maintain without burning out.

Authority builds through consistency, not chaos.

The Real Question of Delivery

Ask yourself:

- Where does my authority land most naturally?

- How do people most easily experience my value?

- What delivery channels feel energizing instead of draining?

The answers will guide you.

In the next chapter, we'll move into **E – Elevation** - where delivery turns into momentum and your authority begins to work for you instead of requiring constant effort.

Clarity defines you.
Ownership grounds you.
Delivery lets the world experience you.

And when those three align, authority becomes undeniable.

Chapter 14: E Is For Elevation

Let Visibility Work for You, Not Against You

This is where everything begins to feel lighter.

Elevation is not about doing more.
It's about allowing what you've built to rise.

This is the final pillar of the Expert Authority Code because it only works when the others are in place. Elevation without clarity creates noise. Elevation without ownership creates insecurity. Elevation without delivery creates inconsistency.

But when all three exist?

Visibility stops being something you chase.
It becomes something that responds to you.

Elevation Is Strategic Visibility - Not Hustle

Let's get one thing straight.

Elevation is not hustle culture dressed up as marketing.

It is not posting every day out of panic.
It is not chasing algorithms.
It is not burning yourself out to stay "relevant."

Elevation is **strategic visibility**.

It's showing up from alignment, not desperation.
It's choosing platforms that match your natural strengths.
It's collaborating instead of grinding alone.
It's letting opportunities find you because your authority is clear and consistent.

This is where my mantra lives comfortably and confidently:

"Remember this - if you're not seen and heard, you're not hired."
– Christine Blosdale

But now it's not pressure.

It's simply truth.

Recognition Comes From Value, Not Volume

Elevation happens when people begin to recognize you.

Not because you're loud - but because you're useful.

Recognition is built through:

- Valuable content that educates and clarifies
- Perspectives that help people think differently

- Consistent messaging that people associate with outcomes

This is how clients begin to find you.

They've seen your content.
They've heard your voice.
They trust your thinking.

By the time they reach out, the sale has already softened.

Attract the Right People, Not Everyone

One of the biggest mistakes I see at this stage is when my gifted clients try to appeal to too many people.

Elevation does not come from being broad.
It comes from being *precise*.

When you release the need to attract everyone and get deeply clear on your niche and audience dynamics, something powerful happens.

The right people feel pulled toward you.

They don't need convincing.
They don't need chasing.

Hallelujah!

They reach out asking for more information.

They raise their hand ready to work with you.

That is your invitation to sell.

Managing Energy Is Part of Elevation

Elevation requires a new level of self-respect.

You cannot scale authority if you're constantly depleted.

This is where working smarter replaces working harder.

That means:

- Honouring rest as a productivity tool

- Delegating tasks that drain you

- Simplifying systems instead of overcomplicating them

Your energy is not unlimited.

Protecting it is not selfish - it's strategic.

Insight Is One of Your Greatest Assets

As an expert, your insight is what sets you apart.

You see patterns.
You sense timing.
You understand nuance.

Elevation asks you to trust that.

This includes trusting your inner authority when making decisions.

Sometimes that means waiting for clarity.
Sometimes it means letting an idea sit before acting.
Sometimes it means saying no to something that looks good on paper but feels off in your body.

Hustle culture teaches urgency.
Authority teaches discernment.

Collaboration Over Isolation

Elevation accelerates in community.

When you don't have a team yet, community is everything.

Build relationships.
Create a circle of trusted people who see you, challenge you, and support you.

And yes - energy exchanges count.

Coaching in exchange for branding.
Visibility support in exchange for admin help.
Mentorship in exchange for photography.

As long as the exchange feels fair and honours both parties' energy, it's valid.

Authority does not grow in isolation.
It grows in connection.

Let Elevation Be Organic

Elevation is not forced.

It's organic.

It looks like:

- Being invited instead of pitching

- Being referred instead of explaining

- Being trusted before being sold

This is what happens when your clarity is strong, your ownership is embodied, and your delivery is consistent.

Visibility becomes a byproduct - not a burden.

A Final Reframe on Elevation

Elevation is not about climbing higher.

It's about standing firmly where you are and allowing the right people to see you.

You don't need to rush this phase.
You don't need to dominate every platform.
You don't need to exhaust yourself to be visible.

You need to be aligned, consistent, and willing to be seen.

That's it.

Before You Move on to The Next Chapter..

Remember, the Expert Authority Code is not about becoming someone else.

It's about becoming *more* of who you already are - clearly, confidently, and visibly.

Clarity shows you who you are.
Ownership anchors you in it.
Delivery lets people experience it.
Elevation allows it to grow.

And when those four work together?

You stop chasing opportunities – and you become one hell of an Expert Authority!

Chapter 15: Make Them Quote You. Becoming Memorable, Referable, and In-Demand

Authority doesn't just live in what you do.

It lives in what people remember about you.

If someone can't easily describe you, repeat your message, or explain why they should refer you, your authority stays stuck in the room you're standing in.

The goal of this chapter is simple:

To help your authority travel.

Why Being Quotable Changes Everything

When people quote you, something powerful is happening.

They're not just listening.
They're internalizing.
They're sharing.

Quotable authority means your message sticks long after the conversation ends. It means people think of you when a problem comes up. It means referrals happen naturally because your language is easy to pass along.

Memorability is not about being clever.

It's about being *clear*.

The Power of a Distinctive Title

One of the fastest ways to anchor expert authority in people's minds is through a clear, distinctive title.

Your title is a mental shortcut.

It answers the question, *"Who are you?"* in seconds.

When I chose **The Expert Authority Coach®**, I wasn't trying to sound fancy. I was creating instant positioning. People immediately know what I help with and why I'm different.

A strong title:

- Creates clarity

- Signals confidence

- Makes you referable

Here are examples of a few titles that I helped develop with my clients that work because they're specific and memorable:

- The ADHD Guy

- The Brain Coach Who Cares

- Transformational Mentor & Empowerment Coach

- Intuitive Past Life Coach

- Serial Entrepreneur

- Aviation Pioneer

Each of these titles gives the audience a hook. They don't explain everything. They explain *enough*.

The mistake many experts make is choosing titles that are vague, generic, or overly complex. If your title needs explaining, it's not doing its job.

Your title should make people say, *"Oh, I know someone who needs you."*

Mantras Make Authority Stick

Titles introduce you.

Mantras make you unforgettable.

A mantra is a short, repeatable phrase that captures your philosophy and reinforces your authority.

One of my favorite ones that I use is simple and direct:

"Remember this - if you're not seen and heard, you're not hired."

That line does a few important things:

- It's easy to remember

- It challenges a belief

- It reinforces my authority positioning

People repeat it because it feels true.

Great mantras don't sound like marketing. They sound like wisdom.

Here are examples of memorable authority-style mantras:

- "Clarity beats clever every time."

- "You don't need more confidence. You need more ownership."

- "Your experience is the qualification."

- "Visibility is not vanity - it's responsibility."

- "If people don't get it, they won't buy it."

A strong mantra becomes shorthand for your work. Over time, people associate that phrase with *you*.

That's authority on autopilot.

Why Simple Language Travels Further

Authority language travels because it's easy to repeat.

Marketing fluff doesn't.

Long explanations. Buzzwords. Overcomplicated messaging. These things die the moment the conversation ends.

But a clean phrase?

That gets remembered. Quoted. Shared.

If you want to test your messaging, ask yourself:

- Could someone repeat this to a friend without notes?

- Would it make sense out of context?

- Does it sound like a human, not a brochure?

If the answer is yes, you're building authority language.

Testimonials Are Authority Echoes

One of the most underused authority tools is letting other people do the talking.

Testimonials, rave reviews, and client stories are not just social proof. They are *authority amplifiers*.

When someone else articulates your value, it lands differently.

A powerful testimonial doesn't just say:
"They were great to work with."

It says:
"Here's who I was before, what changed, and why it mattered."

These stories help future clients see themselves in the transformation. They also reinforce your positioning without you having to say a word.

Referrals Are the Ultimate Authority Signal

When someone refers you, they're putting their reputation on the line.

That's why referrals are one of the strongest indicators of authority.

People refer experts who are:

- Easy to describe

- Clear about who they help

- Known for a specific outcome

If someone struggles to explain what you do, referrals stall.

If your title, message, and mantra are clear, referrals flow.

Make Your Authority Repeatable

Here's the real question this chapter invites you to ask:

If you weren't in the room, could your authority still travel?

Would people know what to say about you?
Would they know who to send your way?
Would they remember how you made them think differently?

That's the work.

Authority that stays locked in your head doesn't scale.
Authority that lives in language does.

So choose your title with intention.
Craft a mantra that sounds like truth.
Collect and share proof that echoes your impact.

Make it easy for people to quote you.

Because when they do, you're no longer chasing opportunity.

You're being talked about.

And that's when authority becomes in-demand.

Chapter 16: Proof Beats Persuasion. Showcasing Your Expert Authority Without Bragging

There comes a point in every expert's journey when trying to convince people starts to feel exhausting.

Explaining.
Justifying.
Proving yourself over and over again.

Here's the shift that changes everything:

When your authority is visible, you don't have to persuade.
Your proof does the talking for you.

And no, showcasing proof does not mean bragging. It means letting evidence speak where words once struggled.

What Authority Proof Really Looks Like

Authority proof is not about shouting your credentials.

It's about *being seen in context*.

It shows up in places where trust is already established, where your expertise is demonstrated naturally, and where others can clearly see the impact of your work.

Some of the most powerful forms of authority proof include:

- A website that clearly positions you as the go-to expert, not a generalist

- Images of you speaking on stage, on panels, or facilitating rooms

- Writing and publishing books, especially bestsellers

- Winning awards from professional organizations

- Being featured in magazines, blogs, or industry publications

- Participating in summits, conferences, and expert panels

- Collaborations and joint ventures with other respected authorities

- Testimonials, case studies, and client success stories

Each one quietly says, *"Others trust this person. You can too."*

Your Website as a Silent Salesperson

Your website should not feel like a resume.

It should feel like a confident introduction.

That's why I recommend to my clients that they feature a short introduction video when visitors come to their website.

Clear messaging.
Strong positioning.
Proof placed intentionally, not buried.

Your homepage alone should answer:

- Who you help

- What you help them do

- Why you're credible to help

When done well, your website becomes one of your strongest authority assets, working for you even when you're offline.

Why Podcast Guesting Is One of the Most Powerful Authority Builders

If I had to choose one visibility strategy that consistently builds trust faster than almost anything else, it would be podcast guesting.

Podcast guesting is not about chasing exposure.
It's about borrowing trust.

When a host invites you onto their show, they are vouching for you. Their audience already trusts them, so that trust transfers to you almost instantly.

And unlike social media, podcast listeners are deeply engaged. Many listen to full episodes. They hear your voice, your energy, your nuance. That kind of connection is rare.

I know this works because I've experienced it personally.

New clients often tell me they discovered me through their favorite podcasts - and that's what inspired them to learn more about my coaching.

Why Podcast Guesting Works So Well

Podcast guesting offers several unique advantages:

- **Warm, targeted audiences**
  Listeners choose shows intentionally. They are already interested in the topic you speak about.

- **High engagement**
  Podcast attention spans are long. Listeners stay with you, often for 30 to 60 minutes.

- **Built-in credibility**
  An invitation is an endorsement. You are introduced as a trusted voice.

- **Cost-effective visibility**
  Most quality podcasts are free to appear on. Be cautious of pay-to-play shows unless there is a clear, proven return.

- **Massive repurposing power**
  One interview can become weeks or months of content across platforms.

Two stats I often share:
A large percentage of podcast listeners consume full episodes, and listeners strongly trust recommendations made during those episodes. Those two facts alone make podcasting a serious authority strategy.

Who Podcast Guesting Is Perfect For

Podcast guesting works beautifully for:

- Coaches and consultants
- Authors and speakers

- Therapists, healers, and practitioners

- Course creators and educators

- Service providers and niche experts

The common thread is simple: you have something valuable to say.

Getting Booked Is About Service, Not Self-Promotion

The biggest mistake experts make when pitching podcasts is making it about themselves.

Hosts don't want you to just promote your business. And your appearance shouldn't feel like an infomercial that's all about you.

They want value for their audience.

A strong pitch clearly communicates:

- Who the episode is for

- What listeners will learn or experience

- Why this conversation matters

Professionalism matters. A concise media kit with suggested topics and questions, and thoughtful preparation make booking you easy and attractive.

Your Media Kit Is an Authority Shortcut

A strong media kit includes:

- A professional headshot

- A short, compelling bio

- Your clear title and positioning

- Suggested interview topics

- Suggested interview questions

- Links to previous appearances

- A simple way to book you

When hosts can immediately visualize the episode, you move to the top of the list.

EXPERT AUTHORITY TIP:

If you need to create a new media kit or if your current one isn't getting you noticed, let's fix that - together. I'll co-create it with you. Simply book a free consultation with me at http://www.ChatWithChristineB.com for more information.

Performance Matters More Than Perfection

When you're on a podcast, how you show up matters as much as what you say.

Clear audio.
Good lighting if video is involved.
A calm, confident presence.

Preparation creates ease. Know your key stories. Have a few quotable soundbites ready. Use simple story structure: problem, process, result.

People remember stories. They repeat results.

Repurposing Turns One Interview Into Many Wins

One podcast interview can become:

- Short video clips

- Quote graphics

- Blog posts

- Newsletter content

- Social media posts

- Lead magnets

- Modules in a course

- Even future book chapters

I've personally turned spoken content into multiple bestselling books. If writing feels hard, speak first. Authority often flows more easily through voice.

Using Tools to Scale Your Guesting Efforts

Manually pitching podcasts can be time-consuming. That's why I use **PodPitch**, a platform that matches experts with podcasts aligned to their expertise.

It pitches you as a potential guest to shows you might never find on your own and it can save you significant time.

Use platforms like this strategically. The tool supports the system, but clarity, preparation, and follow-through are what make it work.

Why Proof Always Outperforms Persuasion

You don't need to convince people you're an authority.

You need to *show them*.

When your expertise is visible through:

- Where you appear
- Who invites you
- What others say about you
- The results you create

Trust forms naturally. Authority becomes assumed, not questioned.

And once proof is in place, marketing feels lighter, conversations feel easier, and opportunities begin to find you.

Because in the end, the most powerful authority doesn't announce itself.

It's recognised.

Chapter 17: Get Paid for What You Know. Monetizing Your Expert Authority

1) Core Service Monetization (the "get paid now" category)

- 1:1 coaching (hourly, package, or retainer)

- VIP days (half-day or full-day intensives)

- Private consulting for businesses or executives

- Done-with-you services (strategy + implementation with client team)

- Done-for-you services (limited spots, premium pricing)

- Audits and reviews (brand audit, funnel audit, messaging audit, offer audit)

- Emergency sessions (48-hour "SOS strategy" premium calls)

Power move: turn your best "quick win" into a paid audit.

2) Signature Program Monetization (the "authority engine")

- Signature group program (your method in 6-12 weeks)

- 90-day accelerator (outcomes-driven with milestones)

- Cohort-based course (live teaching + community)

- Membership (monthly recurring revenue)

- Mastermind (high-touch peer container)

- Certification program (train others in your method)

Power move: name your method and make it a system people can buy into.

---

3) Speaking and Stage Monetization (the "paid to be you" category)

- Paid keynote speaking

- Paid workshops and trainings

- Corporate lunch-and-learns

- Association conferences and industry events

- Local chamber events (often paid or leads to paid work)

- Paid panels and moderated sessions

- Virtual summits as a paid presenter

Extra leverage: speaking fee + back-of-room offer + corporate licensing.

---

4) Publishing Monetization (authority that pays you repeatedly)

- Books (print, ebook, audiobook)

- Companion workbooks and journals

- Special editions (signed copies, premium bundles)

- Bulk book sales to companies or event hosts

- Book-driven funnels (book -> assessment -> call)

- Paid book clubs or "read with me" experiences

- Paid speaking tied to your book (book + keynote package)

Out-of-the-box: license your book content into an internal company training.

5) Digital Products and IP Monetization (make it once, sell forever)

- Mini courses and masterclasses

- Templates (scripts, pitch emails, swipe files, checklists)

- Toolkits (branding toolkit, authority toolkit, media kit kit)

- Playbooks (your method step-by-step)

- Guided audio programs (confidence, mindset, subconscious rewiring)

- Paid webinars (evergreen or live)

- Paid challenges (5-day, 7-day, 21-day)

- Paid assessments (quiz + report + recommendations)

Power move: productize your frameworks into "plug and play" assets.

6) Content Monetization (getting paid for your voice and ideas)

- YouTube monetization (adsense + memberships)
- Podcast monetization (sponsors, dynamic ads, paid episodes)
- Paid newsletter (premium content)
- Subscriptions on platforms (Patreon-style)
- Paid communities (Discord, Circle, Mighty Networks)
- Brand partnerships (aligned only - authority-safe)
- Paid live streams (ticketed)

Out-of-the-box: charge for "office hours" livestreams for members.

---

7) Corporate Monetization (big-budget authority)

- Corporate consulting retainers
- Executive coaching packages
- Team trainings (communication, leadership, mindset, branding)

- Internal workshops + ongoing support

- HR programs (burnout prevention, confidence, productivity)

- Company-wide "masterclass series" contract

- Corporate offsites and retreats

Power move: sell outcomes, not hours. Corporates pay for certainty.

---

8) Licensing and Certification Monetization (the scale category)

- License your framework to other coaches

- Train facilitators to deliver your program

- Certification with renewal fees

- Franchise-style model (careful, but powerful)

- White-label your training for other brands

Out-of-the-box: license your workshop to chambers, councils, and industry groups.

---

9) Affiliate and Referral Monetization (get paid for what you recommend)

- Affiliate links for software/tools that you actually use

- Referral partnerships with service providers (photographers, editors, PR)

- Joint venture promos with revenue-share

- "Tools I use" resource vault with links

Authority rule: only recommend what you'd stake your reputation on.

---

10) Events and Retreats Monetization (transformation premium)

- In-person retreats (high ticket)

- Day retreats or local intensives

- VIP dinners (paid seat + curated networking)

- Paid masterminds in destination locations

- Virtual retreats (ticket + upsell)

Out-of-the-box: "bring-a-friend" retreat pricing to increase conversions fast.

---

11) Authority-Based Product Monetization (beyond services)

- Physical products tied to your method (journals, card decks, planners)

- Branded merchandise only if it reinforces identity (not random)

- Subscription boxes (niche, premium)

- Supplements or wellness products if aligned (with compliance)

Out-of-the-box: limited-run "collector" boxes for superfans.

---

12) Strategic Partnerships and Joint Ventures (authority + distribution)

- Co-created programs with complementary experts

- Bundle or stack giveaways (lead gen + authority boost)

- Summit hosting (speaker fees + sponsor revenue + upsells)

- Partner webinars (split revenue)

- Referral swaps with aligned experts

Power move: collaborate to elevate - while you earn.

---

13) PR and Media Monetization (get paid because you're visible)

- Paid media appearances (rare but possible)

- Paid expert commentary contracts

- "Official expert" roles with brands or networks

- Media training programs you sell (based on your expertise)

- Press-driven inbound leads to premium offers

Out-of-the-box: sell a "Media Magnet" package - guesting + kit + pitch.

---

14) High-Value Access Monetization (people pay for proximity)

- Private Voxer/WhatsApp coaching

- VIP email access

- Priority response tiers

- "Ask me anything" sessions

- Advisory board seat (monthly retainer)

Out-of-the-box: "Authority Hotline" - limited weekly slots.

---

15) Diagnostics and Tools Monetization (people love clarity)

- Paid assessments with personalized scorecards

- Brand archetype / authority zone diagnostics

- Offer clarity diagnostic

- Messaging teardown report

- "Gap analysis" (Authority Gap score)

Power move: diagnostics convert better than generic discovery calls.

16) Micro-Offers That Convert Like Crazy (small yes to big yes)

- $27-$97 quick wins (templates, mini trainings)
- Paid workshops with upsell to program
- Low-ticket "starter kit" to qualify buyers
- Paid challenge with bonus upgrade

Out-of-the-box: "48-hour visibility sprint" micro-offer.

---

17) B2B Content Monetization (sell your brain to businesses)

- Selling internal training packages
- Paid curriculum for industry groups
- Subscription training libraries for teams
- Annual contracts for ongoing content/training

Out-of-the-box: "monthly authority briefing" for leadership teams.

18) Legacy Monetization (future-proof authority income)

- Evergreen funnels (book + course + program)
- Licensing to schools, associations, councils
- Building a "method" brand beyond you

Power move: your method becomes the product, not your time.

A Simple "Authority Monetization Ladder"

1. Paid diagnostic or audit
2. 1:1 package or VIP intensive
3. Signature group program
4. Mastermind or certification
5. Licensing and partnerships

That ladder is how you go from "selling hours" to building an authority business.

Reader Exercise: Design Your Expert Authority Monetization Map

This exercise is not about doing *everything*.

It's about choosing what makes sense for **you**, your energy, and the life you want to build.

Authority monetization works best when it's intentional, aligned, and sustainable.

Take a few minutes with this. Don't overthink it.

Step 1: Name Your Core Expertise

Start here. If you're vague, everything downstream gets muddy.

Complete this sentence:

People come to me because I help them ____________________ so they can

____________________.

Examples:

- "I help business owners clarify their message so they can attract aligned clients."

- "I help leaders manage stress so they can perform at a high level without burnout."

- "I help creatives turn ideas into income so they can build sustainable businesses."

Write your version clearly. This is the engine behind every offer.

Step 2: Choose Your Three Authority Monetization Lanes

You do **not** need all of them.

Circle or write down **three** lanes that feel natural and realistic for you *right now*.

Possible lanes include:

- 1:1 or small group services

- Speaking or training

- Digital products or programs

- Content or media (podcast, video, newsletter)

- Corporate or organisational work

- Publishing (books, guides, workbooks)

- Licensing or certification

- Events or retreats

Ask yourself:

- Which feels easiest to start?

- Which excites me?

- Which supports my lifestyle?

Your authority grows faster when you focus.

Step 3: Match Each Lane to One Clear Offer

Now simplify.

For each of your three lanes, define **one offer only**.

Use this format:

Lane: ___________________

Offer: ___________________

Primary outcome for the client: ___________________

Example:

- Lane: Speaking
  Offer: 90-minute workshop for small businesses
  Outcome: Clear messaging and confidence to show
  up publicly

You are not locking this in forever. You are creating
traction.

Step 4: Check Alignment (The Authority Test)

For each offer, ask:

- Does this reflect my expertise?

- Would I feel confident being known for this?

- Does it support the life I want, not drain it?

- Would I be proud to talk about this repeatedly?

If the answer is no, refine. Authority and resentment cannot coexist.

Step 5: Create One Entry Point

Authority monetization works best when people know *how to begin.*

Choose one simple entry point:

- A free strategy call

- A short paid session

- A workshop or masterclass

- A guide or assessment

This is not about pressure. It's about clarity.

If people don't know the next step, they won't take it.

Step 6: Decide What You Are No Longer Offering

This step is powerful and often overlooked.

Write down one thing you are willing to stop doing or de-prioritise.

- An offer that drains you

- A price that feels too low

- A service that no longer fits

Authority strengthens when you create space.

Final Reflection: Authority Is Meant to Be Paid

Answer this honestly:

If I fully owned the value of what I know, how would my offers look different?

You don't need permission to be paid for wisdom, experience, and results.

You need clarity. You need ownership.
And you need a structure that supports you.

That's what Expert Authority monetization is really about.

Chapter 18: From Scattered to Scalable. Packaging Expertise Into Aligned Offers

Let me start this chapter by putting a new twist on that analogy I told you about earlier and that I use all of the time with my clients.

If I handed you a stapler and said, "Here, make a sandwich," you'd look at me like I'd lost my mind.

Not because you don't know how to make a sandwich. Not because you lack ingredients.

But because a stapler is the wrong tool for the outcome you want.

That's exactly what happens when experts try to sell their brilliance without packaging it properly.

You have the knowledge.
You have the experience.
You have the results.

But if your offers are scattered, unclear, or poorly structured, people don't know how to buy from you.

And confusion never converts.

Why Expertise Alone Doesn't Scale

Most experts don't struggle because they lack value.

They struggle because they've piled everything they know into messy, disconnected offers.

A little of this.
A little of that.
Custom everything.
No clear start or finish.

It feels generous, but it's exhausting.

Scattered expertise drains you.
Packaged expertise scales you.

What an Aligned Offer Really Is

An aligned offer is not just something you sell.

It's something that:

- Reflects your true expertise

- Solves a specific problem

- Has a clear outcome

- Supports the life you want to live

Aligned offers feel clean in your body. You don't dread delivering them. You don't resent the client. You don't constantly re-explain what you do.

They allow you to show up confidently and consistently.

Misaligned offers, on the other hand, create burnout, undercharging, and that constant feeling of "this isn't quite it."

The Core Question Behind Every Aligned Offer

Before we look at examples, ask yourself this:

What do I want to be known for solving?

Not everything you *can* do.

The one thing you want people to hire you for.

That clarity is what allows your offer to become scalable.

Aligned Offer Examples by Profession

Here's what aligned packaging can look like across different fields. Notice how each offer is clear, outcome-driven, and easy to understand.

Business Coach

- Misaligned: "I offer customized coaching on mindset, strategy, systems, and whatever you need."

- Aligned: "A 90-day business clarity and growth accelerator that helps service-based entrepreneurs attract clients and increase revenue."

Divorce Attorney

- Misaligned: "I handle all aspects of divorce cases."

- Aligned: "A step-by-step divorce navigation package for professionals who want clarity, protection, and minimal emotional and financial damage."

Motivational Speaker

- Misaligned: "I speak on motivation, success, and personal growth."

- Aligned: "A keynote on resilience and leadership that helps teams re-engage, reset, and perform under pressure."

Social Media Expert

- Misaligned: "I help with social media management and strategy."

- Aligned: "A 30-day visibility reset that helps small business owners create consistent, confidence-building content without overwhelm."

Leadership Coach

- Misaligned: "I coach leaders on communication, mindset, and performance."

- Aligned: "A 12-week leadership presence program that helps managers lead with confidence, clarity, and authority."

Corporate Management Consultant

- Misaligned: "I consult on operations, change management, and efficiency."

- Aligned: "A leadership alignment and systems optimization engagement designed to improve decision-making and team performance."

Health Expert

- Misaligned: "I help people get healthier."

- Aligned: "A guided wellness reset that helps busy professionals reduce inflammation, improve energy, and regain control of their health."

Fitness Coach

- Misaligned: "I offer personal training and fitness coaching."

- Aligned: "A 16-week strength and vitality program for adults over 40 who want sustainable fitness without burnout or injury."

Real Estate Professional

- Misaligned: "I help people buy and sell property."

- Aligned: "A VIP buyer strategy that helps clients secure the right property before it hits the public market."

See the pattern?

Each aligned offer:

- Names the audience

- Defines the outcome

- Creates confidence

- Makes buying easier

Why Aligned Offers Reduce Burnout

When your offers are aligned:

- You stop over-delivering

- You stop negotiating your worth

- You stop recreating the wheel for every client

Structure creates freedom.

Aligned offers allow you to serve deeply without draining yourself.

They also make your authority visible. People can finally say, *"Oh, I know exactly what you do."*

From Custom Chaos to Confident Structure

This doesn't mean you can't personalize.

It means personalization happens *within a container*.

Your process.
Your method.
Your framework.

That's what people are paying for.

The Authority Shift That Changes Everything

Here's the truth most experts need to hear:

Your job is not to make everything available to everyone.

Your job is to create offers that allow the *right* people to say yes easily.

When you package your expertise into aligned offers, your authority becomes scalable, your income becomes more predictable, and your work starts to feel satisfying again.

That's when you move from scattered to scalable.

And that's when your expertise finally works for you.

Reader Exercise: Design Your First Aligned Offer

This exercise is not about creating the *perfect* offer.

It's about creating a **clear, confident starting point** that reflects your expertise and makes it easy for the right people to say yes.

Give yourself 10–15 uninterrupted minutes.

Step 1: Identify the Problem You Are Best at Solving

Answer this honestly:

People come to me when they are struggling with

______________________________.

Be specific.
Not "life," "business," or "everything."
Examples:

- "Clarity around their message"

- "Navigating a major life transition"

- "Leading with confidence"

- "Building consistent visibility"

- "Regaining energy and focus"

Write one problem only.

Step 2: Define the Outcome You Can Reliably Deliver

Now complete this sentence:

After working with me, people feel or experience

_______________________________.

Think in terms of transformation, not features.

Examples:

- "Clear and confident about what to say and who they serve"

- "Calm, supported, and prepared for the next chapter"

- "More confident making decisions and leading others"

- "Visible and positioned as the expert in their space"

This outcome is what people are buying.

Step 3: Choose the Format That Fits Your Energy

Aligned offers work best when they match how you like to work.

Circle one:

- 1:1 sessions

- Small group program

- Workshop or training

- Short-term intensive (VIP day or sprint)

- Ongoing support or retainer

Ask yourself:

- Can I deliver this without resentment?

- Does this fit my current lifestyle?

- Would I enjoy repeating this offer?

Your energy matters.

Step 4: Define the Container

Every aligned offer needs boundaries.

Fill in the blanks:

- Length of time: _______________________________

- Number of sessions or touchpoints: _______________________________

- Core focus for each phase (if applicable): _______________________________

Clear containers create safety for both you and the client.

Step 5: Name the Offer Simply

Your offer name should be clear before it's clever.

Use this structure if you get stuck:

[Timeframe or format] + [Primary outcome]

Examples:

- "90-Day Authority Accelerator"

- "Clarity and Confidence Intensive"

- "Leadership Presence Program"

- "Visibility Reset Workshop"

If someone hears the name and asks, "What's that?" - refine it.

Step 6: Price for Sustainability, Not Guilt

Ask yourself:

- Does this price respect my time and experience?
- Would I still feel good delivering this six months from now?
- Does this support the life I want to build?

Aligned pricing feels calm, not apologetic.

Step 7: Write Your One-Sentence Offer Statement

This is the sentence you will use everywhere.

I offer _______________________________ *for*
_______________________________ *so they can*
_______________________________.

Example:
"I offer a 12-week leadership presence program for emerging leaders so they can lead with confidence and clarity."

If this sentence feels clean and confident, you're on the right track.

Final Reflection: Alignment Check

Answer this quietly and honestly:

Does this offer reflect who I am becoming, not who I used to be?

If yes, you're ready to move forward.

Your first aligned offer doesn't have to do everything.

It just has to do **one thing well**.

That's how authority is built - one clear, aligned step at a time.

Chapter 19: Authority Is a Long Game (And That's Your Advantage)

If you have deep knowledge, real experience, and a message that genuinely helps people, yet you still feel like you're struggling to be heard, this chapter is for you.

Because here's the truth most people miss.

Expert Authority is not built through noise, trends, or flashy gimmicks. It's built through consistency, positioning, and trust over time. And that means authority favors those who are willing to play the long game.

That's not a disadvantage.

It's your edge.

Why Authority Rewards Patience

In a world obsessed with instant results, viral moments, and overnight success, authority moves differently. It grows steadily. It compounds. And once it's established, it's remarkably resilient.

Authority isn't about chasing attention. It's about becoming familiar. Trusted. Recognized.

People don't hire the loudest expert. They hire the one who feels solid, reliable, and clear.

That kind of trust is earned through repetition and presence, not urgency.

Clarity Creates Momentum That Lasts

One of the biggest mistakes I see is experts constantly changing their message in search of traction. New angle. New hook. New positioning every few weeks.

The problem is not effort.

It's dilution.

When your audience can describe what you do in one sentence, your authority travels without you. Every post, interview, or conversation reinforces the same idea instead of fragmenting it.

Clarity is what allows momentum to build rather than reset.

Visibility Works Best When It's Focused

You do not need to be everywhere to be effective.

In fact, spreading yourself too thin is one of the fastest ways to burn out and disappear. Authority grows faster when you choose one primary place where your people already gather and show up there consistently.

When you focus, you deepen connection.

From there, repurposing becomes your ally. One strong piece of content can live many lives across platforms without requiring more energy from you. The message stays the same. Only the format changes.

That's how visibility becomes sustainable.

Authenticity Is Not a Trend - It's a Trust Signal

People don't connect with perfection. They connect with honesty.

Your lived experience, your detours, your mistakes, your humanity - these are not liabilities. They are evidence.

When you allow people to see the real person behind the expertise, trust accelerates. Authority doesn't weaken when you show your flaws. It strengthens because people recognize themselves in you.

The goal is not to curate a persona.

It's to be believable.

Authority Is Reinforced by Readiness

Having simple tools in place changes how you show up.

A clear media kit.
A short positioning statement.
Defined topics you speak about with confidence.

These aren't just for the outside world. They remind *you* of who you are becoming.

When opportunities appear, you don't scramble. You respond.

And those opportunities build authority faster than sporadic posting ever could.

Listening Is One of the Highest Authority Skills

Experts who scale listen closely.

They notice what questions keep coming up.
They track which messages resonate.
They adapt their offers to real demand instead of assumptions.

This doesn't mean abandoning your expertise. It means translating it.

Small shifts in how you position your work can dramatically expand your reach and income without changing what you actually do.

Authority grows when relevance meets experience.

Consistency Beats Intensity Every Time

One thoughtful piece of content delivered consistently does more than bursts of effort followed by silence.

Authority compounds when your message shows up predictably.

That's why systems matter.

Simple systems for content, conversations, and client journeys allow your authority to grow even when you're resting, traveling, or focusing elsewhere. Consistency builds familiarity. Familiarity builds trust.

Value Always Wins When It's Anchored to What People Care About

At the core, people are drawn to solutions that improve their wellbeing, stability, and relationships.

Whether your work supports health, wealth, connection, or purpose, naming that clearly helps people recognize the value of what you offer.

Authority grows when your message speaks to real needs, not abstract ideas.

Authority Is Felt Through Delivery

Whether you speak, write, record audio, or create video, how you deliver your message matters.

Pacing.
Presence.
Preparation.

You don't need to be theatrical. You need to be intentional.

When your delivery is clear and grounded, people experience competence and confidence without you having to say a word about credentials.

Systems Turn Authority Into Sustainability

At some point, authority must move beyond visibility into structure.

Clear pathways matter.

A conversation starter.
A discovery call.
A signature program or process.

When people know how to move from interest to action,
authority becomes dependable. And dependable
authority spreads through referrals, results, and
reputation.

Authority Evolves - and That's a Good Thing

If something stops resonating, it doesn't mean you failed.
It means you're receiving feedback.

Authority grows through thoughtful evolution.

Small experiments.
Clear communication.
Anchoring change to purpose.

When you explain the "why" behind a shift, people don't
feel confused. They feel included.

And often, the right new audience appears because your
authority is now better aligned with real demand.

The Long Game Is Where Power Lives

Authority is not built in a month.

It's built through clarity repeated, presence sustained, and trust earned.

That's why it lasts.

Start where you are. Commit to what plays to your strengths. Stay visible in ways that feel clean and aligned. Let feedback guide refinement rather than derail you.

Because when your expertise is clear, your delivery consistent, and your positioning honest, visibility stops being a struggle.

It becomes inevitable.

And that's the advantage of playing the long game.

Not louder.
Not faster.
Just unmistakably you.

Chapter 20: Living the Expert Authority Code

By now, you understand something most people never fully grasp:

Authority is not a brand.
It's not a title.
It's not a follower count, a credential, or a viral moment.

Authority is a **way of living**.

The Expert Authority Code was never meant to be a launch strategy you turn on and off.
It was designed to become the *operating system* behind how you think, decide, communicate, and show up — in business and in life.

Because when authority is something you *perform*, it's fragile.
But when authority is something you *embody*, it's unshakable.

This chapter is about that shift.

Not "How do I look like an authority?"
But "Who do I become when authority is my default state?"

Authority Is Not Situational

Most experts unknowingly compartmentalize authority.

They try to sound confident on sales calls
…then shrink in conversations with peers.
They show up boldly online
…then second-guess every decision behind the scenes.
They lead their audience
…but abandon themselves.

True authority doesn't work like that.

You don't *turn it on* for content and *turn it off* for real life.

Authority is who you are when:

- You set boundaries

- You make decisions

- You say no

- You price your work

- You choose rest instead of overexertion

- You trust your knowing without external validation

This is where **C.O.D.E. becomes a way of life**.

C — CLARITY as a Daily Practice

Clarity isn't something you figure out once and move on from.
It's something you *maintain*.

Living in Clarity means:

- You don't overexplain yourself to feel worthy

- You don't chase relevance by diluting your message

- You don't say yes to misaligned opportunities "just in case"

In everyday life, Clarity looks like:

- Knowing when something is a "not for me" — and honoring it

- Communicating directly instead of performing intelligence

- Choosing simplicity over impressiveness

In business, Clarity becomes:

- One clear Authority Zone instead of scattered offers

- Messaging that feels calm, grounded, and unmistakable

- Clients who arrive already understanding your value

When Clarity is embodied, confusion no longer follows you.
People feel you before they understand you.

O — OWNERSHIP as Identity

Ownership is the quiet decision you make *before* the world agrees.

It's the moment you stop asking:
"Am I allowed?"
"Am I ready?"
"Who am I to say this?"

And start asking:
"What do I see that others don't?"
"What responsibility comes with what I know?"
"What happens if I don't lead?"

Ownership in everyday life means:

- You don't downplay your experience to keep others comfortable

- You don't abandon your voice in rooms where you belong

- You don't confuse humility with self-erasure

In business, Ownership shows up as:

- Decisive leadership

- Confident pricing without apology

- Calm certainty even when outcomes are unknown

This is where imposter syndrome loses its grip — not because doubt disappears, but because **leadership outranks fear**.

You stop waiting to be chosen.
You choose yourself — consistently.

D — DELIVERY as Presence, Not Performance

Authority doesn't require perfection.
It requires *presence*.

Delivery is not about sounding polished.
It's about being **felt**.

Living in embodied Delivery means:

- You regulate your nervous system before you regulate your image

- You speak from truth, not from scripts

- You allow pauses, humanity, and imperfection

In daily life, this looks like:

- Speaking clearly instead of filling silence

- Letting your tone match your truth

- Being grounded even when emotions are present

In business, Delivery becomes:

- On-camera confidence without acting

- Messaging that lands because it's real

- Trust built through resonance, not tactics

People don't connect to your expertise alone.
They connect to the *way your expertise feels in their body*.

E — ELEVATION as Alignment

Elevation is what happens when authority stops chasing attention.

You don't need to be everywhere.
You need to be **where you're most powerful**.

Living in Elevation means:

- You choose visibility that supports your nervous system

- You allow collaboration instead of carrying everything alone

- You trust that aligned opportunities respond to embodied authority

In everyday life, Elevation looks like:

- Protecting your energy

- Designing your life to support your leadership

- Saying no to urgency that isn't yours

In business, Elevation creates:

- Effortless visibility

- Referrals without asking

- Clients who seek you out already convinced

When authority is embodied, marketing becomes less about effort and more about *signal*.

The Moment Authority Becomes Permanent

Here's the truth most people never hear:

You don't become an authority because people believe in you.
People believe in you because **you stopped abandoning yourself**.

When C.O.D.E. becomes your way of life:

- Your confidence stabilizes

- Your message simplifies

- Your presence deepens

- Your business becomes sustainable

Authority stops being something you prove.
It becomes something people recognize.

Living the Expert Authority Code

This book was never about making you louder.
It was about making you **truer**.

The Expert Authority Code is not a strategy to apply.
It's a standard to live by.

When you live it:

- Your clarity becomes magnetic

- Your ownership becomes undeniable

- Your delivery becomes trustworthy

- Your elevation becomes inevitable

Authority isn't the destination.
It's the identity you return to — again and again.

And once you live it…

You're no longer asking to be seen.
You're simply standing where you belong.

Chapter 21: An Invitation to Go Further and Mastering Your Expert Authority

If you're still reading, something important has already happened.

You didn't just consume information.

You recognized yourself in these pages.

You felt the pull toward clarity.

You felt the truth of ownership.

You sensed what's possible when your voice, presence, and visibility finally align.

And now there's a quiet question forming:

What would happen if I didn't try to do this alone?

This chapter is an invitation - not because you're missing something, but because you're ready to fully master what you already have.

From Understanding Authority to Living It

Knowing the Expert Authority Code is powerful.

Living it consistently - in your brand, your offers, your messaging, and your income - is transformational.

This is where most experts get stuck.

They know they're meant for greater visibility.
They feel the pull to lead.
They have the experience, the insight, and the heart.

But translating that into:

- A powerful personal brand

- Clear, signature offers

- Aligned and scalable income

- Unshakable confidence in being seen

…that's where the shift needs to happen.

And that's where the right guidance makes all the difference.

That's where I come in.

An Invitation To Go Further

Let me speak to you directly.

I'm Christine Blosdale - also known as The Expert Authority Coach ® - and my life is dedicated to helping people like you stop circling their potential and start claiming their place as the go-to authority in their field.

I've spent over 25 years in media, coaching, branding, and authorship.

But more importantly…

I've helped hundreds of entrepreneurs, coaches, authors, and thought leaders elevate their visibility, amplify their message, and reach goals they once believed were out of reach.

I know what it takes to be seen - because I've lived it from every angle.

Early in my career, I created content for global powerhouses like America Online and Microsoft, learning firsthand how messaging, media, and positioning shape perception and influence.

I bring that media savvy and marketing magic into everything I do today.

My coaching style is simple, easy, and fun - and most importantly, effective.

I don't believe in cookie-cutter strategies.

I believe in you.

Your voice.
Your story.
Your authority.

That's why everything I do is customized around your unique strengths, goals, and vision - so your brilliance doesn't get lost trying to sound like someone else.

My mission is to help you rise with clarity, confidence, and the mindset of an Expert Authority.

Two Ways to Go Further

If you feel the pull to deepen this work, I've made it easy for you to take the next step.

You're invited to visit my website at **ExpertAuthorityCoach.com**, where you'll find two options.

1. Book a FREE Expert Authority Consultation

This is a no-pressure quick conversation designed to support you.

We'll explore:

- Where you are now
- Where you want to go
- What's been holding you back
- What's ready to emerge

You'll leave with clarity - whether we work together or not.

Sometimes, one aligned conversation is enough to unlock your next level.

To book that free chat with me simply go to ChatWithChristineB.com

2. Join My Authority Accelerator Program

If you're ready for true transformation, this is where we go all in.

Inside my Authority Accelerator Program, we:

- Build a powerful, authentic brand that reflects who you truly are
- Clarify and refine your signature offers
- Identify aligned income possibilities that feel expansive, not exhausting
- Create step-by-step guidance so you're never guessing your next move

This isn't about hustling harder.

It's about becoming unmistakable.

To learn more visit 90DayExpertAuthority.com

Clients often tell me this work doesn't just change their business - it changes how they see themselves.

And that's when everything accelerates.

This Is Not the End of the Book - It's the Beginning of Your Authority

You don't need more credentials to begin.

You don't need permission.

You don't need to wait until you feel "ready."

You're already closer than you think.

If this book resonated with you, it's because your authority has been quietly waiting to be claimed.

So consider this chapter an open door.

Walk through it when you're ready.

I'll be there to guide you — every step of the way.

Visit **ExpertAuthorityCoach.com**

Book your free consultation.

Explore the Authority Accelerator.

And let's turn what you already know…into the authority you live.

Chapter 22: Your Expert Authority Toolkit. Resources I Use and Highly Recommend

Becoming a recognized Expert Authority doesn't happen by accident. It happens when you combine clarity, consistency, visibility—and the *right tools*.

Over the years, I've tested, tried, invested in, and fallen in love with resources that genuinely support building authority, saving time, increasing visibility, and generating revenue. This chapter features the exact books, programs, platforms, and equipment I personally use and confidently recommend to my clients.

These are not "nice to haves." They're *needle movers*.

Important Disclosure

This chapter contains a few affiliate links, which means I may earn a commission if you choose to join a program. But know this - I truly love and use all of these resources anyway, and I recommend them because they work. I only share tools I'd confidently tell my closest friends and clients to use.

Start Here: Work Directly With Me

FREE 30-Minute Expert Authority Consultation ($250 Value)

If you're tired of wasting time (and money) trying to figure out the smartest way to build and scale your Expert Authority, this is where you start. This is a real strategy call with me - your very own personal Expert Authority Coach - and yes, it's **absolutely FREE**.

☞ Book your free consultation at ChatWithChristineB.com

Signature Coaching Programs

My 90-Day Expert Authority Accelerator Program

This is my flagship coaching experience for entrepreneurs, leaders, and visionaries who are done playing small.

Inside this subscription-based program, you'll receive:

- Weekly private coaching sessions

- Personal branding & visibility strategies

- Podcasting, social media, publicity & messaging support

- 24/7 access to my Masterclass Vault (20+ programs)

This is where clarity, confidence, and consistency come together - fast.

☞ Learn more and sign up at
90DayExpertAuthority.com

The Expert Authority Mastermind For Women In Business

If you're ready for momentum, collaboration, and next-level growth - this is your place.

This isn't just another women's group. **It's a launchpad.**

Every other week you'll experience:

- Strategic insights of private coaching

- High-level group collaboration

- Visibility tools and authority positioning

☞ Explore the Mastermind (or take it for a test drive) at
https://www.christineblosdale.com/mastermindbychristine

Books I've Written to Support Your Authority Journey

The Social Media and Branding Survival Guide

Digital Marketing So Irresistible Even Your Ex Will Want to Follow You!

My #1 bestselling book on branding, visibility, and magnetic marketing.

☞ Get your copy on Amazon: https://amzn.to/3Yyn5O3

Podcastonomics: Unlocking the Secrets of Profitable Podcasting for Beginners

Your backstage pass to launching, growing, and monetizing a podcast—without overwhelm.

☞ Grab it here: https://amzn.to/3LlxOZi

Grab That Microphone: Your Guide to Becoming an In-Demand Podcast Guest

If you want podcast guesting to become a serious authority and lead-generation channel, this book is your roadmap.

☞ Get your copy here: https://amzn.to/4qiTOmI

Free Planners & Webinars

FREE ChatGPT Money-Making Activities Planner

This isn't a task tracker—it's a profit driver.
Log into ChatGPT, answer a few prompts, and walk away with a customized daily action plan built to grow your authority *and* your income.

☞ Get it FREE:
https://mailchi.mp/acdf9cb2a5cb/chatgpt_planner

The Top 10 Things You Should Be Doing to Promote Your Business

Instant FREE access to my top visibility strategies to attract clients and grow your brand.

☞ Watch it free: https://mailchi.mp/8c8f3dad3fab/the-top-10-things-you-need-to-do-to-promote-your-business

Book Like A Boss

My all-in-one scheduling, payment, and sales platform. I use it to book sessions, sell programs, and manage my business with ease.

☞ Start your FREE trial:
https://www.blab.co/pricing/freelancer?fpr=christine

Podbean Podcast Hosting (30-Day Free Trial)

Simple, affordable, beginner-friendly podcast hosting—
with monetization options.

☞ Try it free: http://podbean.com/Christine

AI, Video & Content Creation Tools

Descript

AI-powered audio and video editing that makes content
creation ridiculously easy.

☞ Try it free: https://get.descript.com/jvudgk834wf4

Video To Blog

Turn videos into high-quality blog posts automatically.
One of my absolute favorite time-saving tools.

☞ Free trial: https://www.videotoblog.ai/?via=christine

Wistia Video Marketing Platform

Create, host, embed, and analyze your videos beautifully—all in one place.

☞ Try Wistia free for 2 weeks:
https://try.wistia.com/christine

Movavi Video Editor

My go-to editor for YouTube and everyday video creation. Intuitive, fast, and powerful.

☞ Try Movavi free: https://www.mvvitrk.com/D6gGJv

Forms, Automation & Design

Fillout

A powerful (and free) form builder I use for podcast guest releases and workflows.

☞ Try it free: https://www.fillout.com/?ref=cblosdale

Canva Pro

My daily design tool for thumbnails, graphics, social posts, and more.

☞ Try Canva Pro free for 30 days: https://partner.canva.com/c/1787857/647168/10068

Podcast Equipment I Trust

Shure MV7 Microphone

My top-choice microphone for podcasting and professional audio quality.

☞ Get it here: https://amzn.to/3yWbOeH

Your Expert Authority isn't built on hustle alone- it's built on smart systems, aligned tools, and consistent action.

You don't need *everything* in this chapter.
But you do need **the right next thing**.

Choose what supports your vision, your energy, and your next level—and let your authority do the rest.

Your Authority Is Already Inside You

If there's one thing I hope you take away from this book, it's this:

You were never meant to chase credibility.
You were meant to *claim it*.

Your Expert Authority isn't something you earn someday when you're "ready enough," visible enough, or confident enough. It already lives inside you—shaped by your experiences, your lessons, your failures, your wins, and the people you are meant to serve.

This book wasn't written to turn you into someone else. It was written to help you **fully step into who you already are** - with clarity, courage, and conviction.

You now have the code.
The mindset shifts.
The strategies.
The tools.

The only thing left is action.

So speak up.

Show up.

Be seen.

The world doesn't need another watered-down version of you—it needs your voice, your perspective, and your authority exactly as it is.

And when doubt creeps in (because it will), remember this:

Authority isn't about being perfect.

It's about being present, intentional, and unapologetically you.

Your journey doesn't end here.

It begins right now.

—

Christine Blosdale - The Expert Authority Coach™

ExpertAuthorityCoach.com

Final Chapter: This Is Where It Begins

If you've made it to the end of this book, CONGRATULATIONS! Something has already shifted.

You may not even have the words for it yet, but you can feel it.

The confusion that once clouded your direction has started to clear.
The hesitation that once held you back doesn't feel as strong as it did before.

And the idea of stepping into your authority no longer feels like something reserved for "other people."

It feels possible.

Because now, you understand something most people never fully grasp.

Authority is not something you wait for.
It's not something you are given.
And it's not something reserved for the loudest or the most visible.

Authority is something you claim.

Throughout this book, you've seen what happens when clarity replaces confusion, when ownership replaces hesitation, when delivery becomes grounded instead of performative, and when visibility becomes aligned instead of exhausting.

You've seen the pattern.

You've seen the path.

And more importantly, you've seen yourself in it.

That matters.

Because this was never about turning you into someone else.

It was about helping you recognize who you already are.

Your experience is not random.
Your knowledge is not accidental.
Your perspective is not insignificant.

Everything you've lived, learned, navigated, and overcome has shaped your authority.

Not someday.

Now.

You do not need more credentials to begin.
You do not need permission to move forward.
You do not need to wait until you feel completely ready.

Because readiness doesn't come before action.

It comes from it.

So if you've been standing at the edge, wondering when the right moment will arrive, let me be clear.

This is the moment.

Not a perfect moment.
Not a fearless moment.
But a real one.

And real is more than enough.

The truth is, your authority does not grow when you stay hidden.

It grows when you speak.
When you show up.
When you allow yourself to be seen in the fullness of what you know and who you are becoming.

Will there be moments of doubt? Absofrigginlutely.
Will fear still show up? Of course.
Will everything feel perfectly aligned right away? No.

But none of that disqualifies you.

Because authority is not built in the absence of fear.

It is built in the presence of truth.

Every time you choose to communicate clearly instead of overcomplicating…

Every time you choose to own your experience instead of downplaying it…

Every time you choose to show up instead of shrinking back…

You strengthen your authority.

And over time, those choices compound.

People begin to recognize you.
They begin to trust you.
They begin to refer you.
They begin to choose you.

Not because you chased them.

But because **you became unmistakable**.

That is the work.

And now, it is yours to do.

As you move forward, remember this:

You don't need to be everywhere.
You need to be consistent.

You don't need to impress everyone.
You need to be clear to the right people.

You don't need to become someone new.
You need to fully stand in who you already are.

That is where your authority lives.

And that is where your next level begins.

If you feel called to go further, to deepen this work, and to fully step into your authority with clarity, structure, and support, you are invited to work with me.

This is the work I do every day.

I help entrepreneurs, coaches, authors, and thought leaders move from uncertainty to clarity, from hesitation to ownership, and from being overlooked to becoming the go-to authority in their space.

If that resonates with you, you can learn more and explore ways to work together by visiting ExpertAuthorityCoach.com.

But whether you choose to take that step or continue on your own, know this:

You already have what you need to begin.

You always did.

The difference now is that you see it.

So speak.

Show up.

Be seen.

Because the world does not need another watered-down version of you.

It needs your voice.
Your perspective.
Your authority.

Exactly as it is.

And once you fully step into that…

You won't just be seen.

You will be chosen.